THE KITCHEN AND BATHROOM BOOK

José Manser writes regularly for *Ideal Home* and the *RIBA Journal*, and she contributes articles to *Design Magazine, Building Design*, the *Observer Colour Magazine*, the *Guardian* and others. She has written two books – *Bathrooms* (Studio Vista, London 1969), and *Planning Your Kitchen* (Design Council, London 1976) with her architect husband Michael as co-author.

JOSÉ MANSER

THE KITCHEN AND BATHROOM BOOK

Planning & Decorating your two most functional rooms

Pan Original
Pan Books London and Sydney

Acknowledgements

I should like to thank the following people. Kindly
and uncomplainingly they allowed Clifford Jones, the
photographer, and me to invade their homes and take
photographs of their bathrooms or kitchens or, in
several cases, both:

Anne and Tony Barnes,
Michael Baumgarten,
Madeleine Berry,
Chloe Cheese,
Angela Chidgey,
Joy and John Dievel,
Barry Gray,
Myrna and John Guest,
Andrew and Bernice Holmes,
Peter King,
Dieter Klein,
Moira and John McConnell,
Veronique and David Richmond,
Sue and Brian Taggart,
Jon Wealleans.

Also thanks to the following who were generous
enough to give us photographs of kitchens or
bathrooms:

Peter Bell,
The Design Council,
Nicholas Grimshaw and Partners,
Designers Guild,
Bernard Hunt,
Jan Kaplicky,
Ron and Barbara Nixon,
Anne and James Pilditch,
Jeremy Rewse-Davies,
John Thompson
Barry Weaver.

●

First published 1982 by Pan Books Ltd,
Cavaye Place, London SW10 9PG
© José Manser 1982
ISBN 0 330 26579 2
Printed and bound in Great Britain by
Morrison & Gibb Ltd, London and Edinburgh

Contents

INTRODUCTION 6

Introduction

Consider for a moment the amount of advertising that is concerned with equipment and furnishings for kitchens and bathrooms. Women's magazines and newspaper colour supplements would suffer grievous losses without it. And to some extent it has built up an unfortunate image of unattainable perfection which can be the cause of much unnecessary discontent.

The reasons for this concentration of advertising is clear. Kitchens and bathrooms are of prime importance to a household. They are – at least in the state of sophistication and high living standards reached by western countries – absolutely essential. No household can be without them. All the same, I believe very strongly that no one needs (or even wants) half the items which we are assured are essential to our well-being in these areas. On the other hand, many families' lives could be made easier and more comfortable if some hard thought were given to their planning arrangements, for a bathroom or kitchen that is awkward to use, difficult to clean and otherwise badly planned can affect everyone in the household at some time during the day. It can make them tired, depressed, frustrated and bad tempered, none of these particularly desirable moods in which to go out and face the world.

I also think that life is sweetened if one's home looks good. Sometimes good looks follow naturally on thoughtful planning and careful choice of individual items, as I will explain later. Sometimes, though, they are dependent on additional factors such as agreeable colour schemes, well-designed chairs and attractive accessories. But each and every one of these things is important if you are striving to achieve the best possible end result.

It is difficult to consider creating a new kitchen or bathroom, or even revamping an existing one, without the word money looming large. There is no doubt it can cost a great deal to carry out a project of this sort. Services such as plumbing and electrics are expensive to install or alter, trades such as joinery, bricklaying and decorating are highly priced, and the cost of new equipment, even of the cheapest variety, quickly mounts up to sickeningly large totals. Take heart. It is *still* possible, if you plan carefully, consider your own genuine needs (as opposed to needs you have been brainwashed into thinking you have) and are prepared to carry out the work in stages, to achieve your ends within your means.

It is certain that no household needs all the items so enthusiastically promoted as being indispensable by the manufacturers, and it is important to assess your requirements with soul-searching honesty. A deep-freeze, for instance, when you live in a large city where

Despite many enthusiastic predictions, the design and equipment of kitchens and bathrooms has changed remarkably little over the past ten years. The plug-in kitchen, computer-controlled home shopping centre and plastic-pod bathroom have all been described but remain mainly figments of somebody's imagination. But, whilst not being shatteringly innovatory, there are some excellent, very modern bathrooms and kitchens to be seen, even if some exist only as prototypes.

1. was designed by George Fejer and shown in an exhibition at the Design Centre in London. As well as curved floor-to-ceiling laminated plastic capsules which house wash bowl, bidet, lavatory, cupboards and bath, it features finger-sensitive buttons which operate water, temperature and lights – no breathtaking advance in all that, admittedly, but a nice piece of design all the same.

2. is not a prototype but a kitchen designed by architect Brian Taggart for his own home. While paying due respect to the Victorian architecture of the house – leaving mouldings, room shapes and windows untouched – he has inserted a crisply modern high tech style kitchen/dining room into the two ground-floor rooms. Chromed wire mesh shelves hang on the cream-painted walls, the unit doors are made from aluminium sandwich construction panels, trimmed with black plastic, and there are red laminated plastic work surfaces. An island unit, foreground, houses the gas hob which has its pipes exposed in true high tech style.

1

Though layout and equipment used in kitchens has changed little in recent years, style is another matter. A whole generation, quite unshackled by any prescriptive approach to decoration, is tackling the kitchen with the verve and freshness it gives to any other design job. This room, for instance, was given drama and vitality by its owner, Sonnie Howson's, highly original approach. Brilliant red paint on practically every paintable surface, plus black wall tiles, have been used to make a singular and successful kitchen interior.

certain shops are open until late at night and you grow no abundance of garden produce? A dishwasher when there are just two in the family and you rarely entertain? A kitchenful of new units when the existing ones are solid and capacious and could easily be refurbished? A bidet which you have no intention of using? Do not misunderstand me. I am not saying no one needs a deep-freeze, dishwasher, new kitchen units, or bidet. Plenty of people do. But do *you*?

The other question to ask yourself is, do you need them now? It is perfectly possible, indeed it is sensible, to plan a kitchen or bathroom with future requirements in mind. So, for instance, you cannot afford an automatic washing machine now, but you have left space for it where plumbing is conveniently located. You cannot

discussed or shown in the appropriate chapters.

Are there many new and exciting ideas in kitchen and bathroom design at the moment? On the whole there are not. There *are* areas where things are changing, of course, but they tend to be peripheral rather than mainstream.

In the kitchen, for instance, much electrical equipment is now operated electronically. This means that there are washing machines with precise control over such variables as time, temperature and agitation; and there are cookers with electronically controlled heat settings which fluctuate according to the needs of a recipe throughout cooking. But compared with products in other fields, the level of sophistication and advance is fairly low, and even the touch controls which some manufacturers bravely introduced (no knob, just a marked area on a flat panel which you touched to operate a cooker or hob) were withdrawn by most companies almost before consumers had registered their existence. A pity, this, because they were far superior in appearance and ease of cleaning to the sundry knobs and switches with which appliances are generally fitted, and the few which have stayed the course are welcome indeed. Generally speaking, though, in the kitchen, the great potential of microchip technology remains as yet largely unexploited. Instead, manufacturers are diverting our attention with the joys of colour. Coloured (and matching) ovens, hobs, dishwashers, washing machines and refrigerators are all available, and though the colour ranges are a little limited and conservative, they open up quite interesting new possibilities in kitchen design.

The prefabricated plastics bathrooms which were heralded as instant answers to the problem of house conversion some years ago have not developed and become part of general building or DIY practice, although every now and again some manufacturer tries without much success to rouse interest in yet another prototype. And almost inevitably this sinks rapidly into the oblivion which has engulfed all its predecessors. Nor does the free-standing packaged kitchen which some people were predicting, destined to be plonked down in any part of the house with arteries connecting it to services, show serious signs of materializing.

Bathroom equipment manufacturers are teetering on the brink of radical new designs in the electronics field, but while innovative designers have produced prototype bathrooms for exhibitions where the taps and WC flushes are operated electronically, no manufacturers had at the time of writing put their money into the large-scale manufacture of such things. But undoubtedly they will. Let us hope that this will at least help to eliminate

afford *all* the units you really need, but you have started with a few, have designed the kitchen with space for more, and will add them as finances allow and growing needs demand. Wall tiling, a second wash bowl, a bidet, a built-in dressing shelf around the wash bowl — any number of things such as these can be planned for and acquired over a period of time.

There are other ways in which good kitchens and bathrooms can be made without excessive expenditure. Various ideas such as the rearrangement of old equipment rather than the purchase of new, the refurbishing of old kitchen units and their mating and matching with a few new ones, the transformation which can be effected by colour and the simple addition of a few extra, but vital, shelves and cupboards, will all be

some of the badly designed taps which dominate the market. You do not agree that taps are badly designed? Have a look at the ones in your own bathroom and (although these may be a little better) kitchen. Do they have awkward angles both in their own shapes and in the shape in which they rise from the wash bowl? The chances are they do, and that this area is therefore difficult to clean and the recipient of hard water deposits. Do they have ugly knobs of coloured acrylic, slippery and difficult to grasp with a soapy hand? Remember the simple cross-head tap which was both functional and good looking? It is virtually unobtainable now except as an expensive reproduction manufactured abroad.

Instead, the showrooms are full of products which, while they look vulgarly bright and gleaming, and may have instant sales appeal for some, are not conducive to easy cleaning (which should surely be an important consideration) and are awkward to use and grossly shaped.

Many kitchen units have equally serious design faults, and Continental manufacturers are the original culprits. Their predilection for heavily curved and carved door fronts has produced some bulky dirt-collecting examples which would dominate and darken small kitchens in a most depressing way. This is an area where British products are on the whole simpler and better, though a few misguided manufacturers have leapt on to the foreign bandwagon.

The message is clear. Beware any equipment, whether it is cupboards, taps, sanitaryware or cookers, which is not easy to clean. Inspect any intended purchase minutely for tight crevices, joints and convoluted knobs, and for an overabundance of poor-quality chrome. Reject anything which cannot be easily cleaned.

Apart from the influence of chip technology on kitchen equipment there has been one other new development. It is in the bathroom. Just as you fit out your kitchen, so you may now fit out your bathroom with built-in cupboards and shelves. Not ideal for a small room since it takes up too much space, this sort of arrangement can be excellent in an older, more roomy house where, as well as providing lots of storage, it will conceal ill-plastered or otherwise less than perfect walls, hide any ugly plumbing pipes and make for a general air of order and tidiness.

That is, always supposing you like that type of look in your bathroom. For again, other changes have been taking place in the world of interior design and decoration, and apart from a variety of styles in between, this has polarized into two extreme fashions (not just in

1. Wood is a beautiful material with an emotional appeal which makes it highly suitable for kitchen use. It is unfortunate that many manufacturers have seen fit to ruin its natural properties with their overworked and ugly products. This kitchen, made by Michael Baumgarten for his flat in a converted warehouse, shows wood at its simple best, with maple top and drainer above beech-fronted cupboards.

2. It has always been possible to bring colour into a kitchen with paint, wallpaper, curtains and laminated plastic, but too often an aura of clinical gloom was introduced by the stark white doors of the dishwasher, washing machine, refrigerator and so on. Some manufacturers are now helping to improve matters by producing coloured ranges. The colours are rather limited as yet and not of the most exciting – green and gold predominate – but this bright red is a sign of braver things to come. Its manufacturer produces cookers, hobs, refrigerators and washing machines in the same colour. If you feel like buying the lot, remember that it might inhibit your choice of kitchen colour schemes when you come to redecorate.

1

It is a sad fact that not all progress is for the better, and this applies in too many cases to modern tap design. There are very few first-class examples and now manufacturers, apparently waking up to the fact that they are not giving their customers what they want, have given up the struggle and started harking back to the past. Two excellent examples of reproduction Edwardian taps are shown here (not all are so accomplished and some are positively gruesome), which, although rather expensive, would contribute a great deal of style to any type of bathrooom.
1. shows a simple stand-up tap with a chrome finish, and 2. shows a brass bath and hand-shower mixer with a simple and graspable lever control. The brass is lacquered for easy cleaning. It seems a pity that so few manufacturers are able to produce really modern designs to compete with these eminently satisfactory old-fashioned designs.

bathrooms and kitchens but in every part of the house).

At one end of the scale there is the soft, slightly untidy and woody look in which the kitchen apes the country farmhouse (*especially* so in the heart of the city) and which places the kitchen in the womb-like, pivot-of-the-home category. Its bathroom manifestation takes the form of such things as stripped pine washstands, wooden WC seats and free-standing baths. At the other end of the scale there is the fashion called 'high tech' which could not be more different. This features components straight from the factory floor, the hospital operating theatre or the warehouse, translated into the domestic scene. Not surprisingly it is, to date, rather more popular for kitchens than for bathrooms.

The only other real development to affect kitchens and bathrooms is the general and essential emphasis on energy conservation. The world's diminishing resources and rising costs have at last caused us to cut our cloth accordingly, and in the two rooms in question this has resulted in extra insulation for energy consuming equipment, assisted circulation in ovens which reduces cooking times and temperature levels, more interest in showers since they use far less water than baths (and in shower units equipped with instantaneous water heaters) and the careful insulation of hot water tanks by householders.

Before you rush into redesigning your room (whether it is a kitchen or bathroom) or even building a new one, remember that it may be necessary to comply with certain statutory requirements.

If the room is to take the form of an extension, and is over 15% of the overall size of the house you need such permission. And if you are making any structural alterations at all – knocking down internal walls, rearranging the plumbing, moving windows, etc. – you will always need to have your ideas looked at and approved by the local building inspector or, in the London area, the district surveyor, one of whose tasks is to ensure the safety and sanitariness of both your own and your neighbours' properties. So consult the appropriate departments at your local authority offices *before* you start work.

Then there is the question of home improvement grants. These are of various types, some statutory, some discretionary, and may be available if you are building a kitchen or bathroom where once there was none, if you lack amenities such as a hot water supply, or if you are doing conversion work. Get full details from your local authority and make your application before you start work. Grants cannot be given once the work has commenced. If you are going to employ an architect, he or she will deal with any applications regarding planning and building regulations. In fact, this is a good point at which to define the architect's role. For kitchens and bathrooms are often difficult to plan and expensive to equip and in many cases it is well worth while to employ an architect to ensure you are spending your money in a sensible, logical fashion.

An architect may be a man or a woman (though for simplicity I shall refer to 'him'). He is trained, as no other professional person is, to plan the use of space in the most economical, logical and aesthetically pleasing fashion. He will incorporate the necessary technical services (heating, fume extraction, plumbing, etc.) in an efficient, functional and economical way, and then supervise the construction of his scheme, be it kitchen or power station or any size of building in between, to the satisfaction of his client. Besides all this he is commonly required to act as go-between, whipping boy, financial adviser and occasional labourer.

Not all architects are good in all these roles. Some are. Choose yours carefully. In the context of kitchen and bathroom design, look at work which has been done for friends, look for schemes you admire in the home magazines and, best of all, consult the client's advisory service of the Royal Institute of British Architects, 99 Portland Place, London W1, who will give you a list of potentially suitable architects in your area. But do not take their descriptions on trust. Look at the candidates' previous work, talk to their clients. That way your choice is likely to be a good one.

An interior designer is not normally qualified to cope with structural work, such as a new extension or large scale alterations. He could, however, undertake the replanning or refurbishing of an existing kitchen. To find the best person for the job consult the Design Council, 28 Haymarket, London SW1, for a list of possible candidates and then – as with an architect – make your own careful inspection of previous work.

Do not, incidentally, assume that a woman will design a better kitchen or bathroom than a man. She may, but not necessarily so. A good designer is a good designer, of either sex.

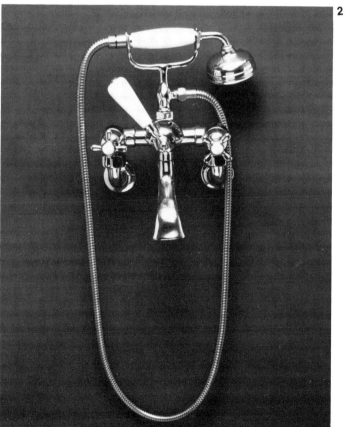

2

13

KITCHENS

Equipment

When you are planning a new kitchen or refurbishing an old one, the first decisions that have to made are about what you are going to put in it; which items of equipment, and then which brand and which models of those particular items. The choice is bewildering, so brace yourself to bring a really cool and critical mind to the job.

Think of all the things that may be involved. Kitchen units, of course, and then the following: cooker, sink, refrigerator, freezer, washing machine, tumble-drier, dishwasher, microwave oven, sink grinder, extractor fan and hood – and that is before you even consider such small, free-standing items as coffee grinders, food mixers, electric kettles and so on.

But do you need them all? Note, I say 'need', not 'want'. As I mentioned in the previous chapter, advertising has gulled many of the more impressionable amongst us into believing that it is really our right to possess every single one of the above items. But if it is a workable and attractive kitchen you are after, you will work out your genuine needs before surrounding yourself with a plethora of goods, some of which you rarely use. That way you will not only cut down on expense but you will also avoid clutter and confusion in

what is inevitably one of the busiest and most frequently used rooms in the house.

By saying this I am not in any way advocating a streamlined, clinical-looking kitchen as the only answer (though for some people it may well suit the book), but just pointing out that everything you plan for should have its purpose and pay for the space it occupies in terms of the amount of times it is used.

For example, an excess of cupboards in the shape of expensive units can simply encourage the hoarding of unnecessary junk which will languish there for years until somebody has the energy or the willpower to dump it. Or conversely, superfluous cupboards can remain empty, their only apparent function to act as wall coverings rather like hyper-expensive wallpaper. What a waste of money! So assess your needs realistically, remembering that new acquisitions very often replace old ones which should then be thrown away. If you are just starting off family life, with one or two small children and perhaps another planned, you will be sensible to allow for a few more possessions than you have. If, on the other hand, your grown-up children have just left home and the household has contracted (perhaps you

Interior fittings should be well thought-out to be really useful. 1. is a deep drawer built-in below the oven for saucepans, with a central division to keep the contents neat. 2. is a pull-out rubbish bin of sensible proportions and with a lid to prevent smells.

3. This kitchen is made from a standard range of units which have been designed with the current popularity of wooden kitchens very much in mind. The backs, solid doors, drawer fronts and frames are in old seasoned pine, and there are white melamine-veneered chipboard structures. The emphasis is on quality (drawers are made of solid wood and dovetailed), and detailing, such as the wooden handles, is excellent. Despite period looks, the interiors are fitted to a high modern standard.

have moved into a flat, rather than the house, and it is for that you are planning a kitchen), you will be stupid to do so.

And what about all those gleaming pieces of machinery which leer so seductively from the glossy coloured magazine pages? There is that huge trunk-shaped freezer, for instance, which the salesman assures you will save a fortune in petrol bills to the shops, meat bought in daily consumable quantities, etc. Well, this fortune will not be saved if you live close to a major shopping street, if you are a small family who entertain very little, and if your back garden does not yield quantities of soft fruit and vegetables. You would be better off with a reasonably proportioned refrigerator/freezer, leaving the other great yawning monster for the countrywoman with a large family and prolific garden. Nor will you want a double oven if your entertaining is normally done on a small scale, a tumble-drier if you have both indoor and outdoor hanging space for wet clothes, or a large and expensive washing machine if what you are planning is a small weekday *pied-à-terre* with your main home in the country. There is a great deal in favour of each and every one of the appliances mentioned, and there are some households which will run much more smoothly if they have each and every one of them. But for most households, this is not true. Think about how you live, and how you intend to live over the next ten years (it may not work out quite as planned, but you can try), then make your purchases accordingly.

To help you, there follows a brief description of what is available, what is new and what is best – best meaning best designed and best value.

Kitchen units

If you intend to buy new kitchen storage cupboards, they will either be custom designed (by you or your architect), or they will be bought from a proprietary range of which there are many on the market. It is also possible that you are considering some hybrid arrangement made up of old cupboards originally intended for some completely different use, as described under the heading 'The non-kitchen' (page 80).

Proprietary brand units

These can either be bought ready-made, and probably installed by a representative of the manufacturer, or they can be self-assembled. They will generally consist of variations on the following components: floor cupboards, wall cupboards, tall (broom) cupboards, housing for cookers and refrigerators and floor cup-

boards to take sink units. Many of the floor-standing units incorporate drawers of varying depths.

Within that simple list lies a multitude of different possibilities, immensely boosted and stimulated in recent years by the influx of products from Europe. Not all of these are good. Some are overdecorated and vulgar beyond belief, but at their best (generally from Italy) they are of superb design and have pushed British manufacturers into reconsidering and improving their often tired and uninspired-looking ranges.

A big change has been the transferral of popularity from laminated plastics finishes to wood finishes. Laminated plastics (Formica, Melamine, etc.) are still available in plenty, of course, and on many of the top-quality ranges they look and function well, but the feeling for wood is strong. There is oak, cherry and pine, the latter sometimes stained in soft colours. Ash is a beautiful wood which in at least one manufacturer's range is available lacquered in strong pure colours, and amongst the cheaper products good old unpainted whitewood allows the more creative kitchen planner to decorate in an imaginative and individual fashion. A splendid range from Italy has toughened glass doors set

3

into hand-finished wooden frames, and one of the best English ranges is also available with glass doors.

Some manufacturers have tried to get the best of both worlds by facing their units with laminated plastics which simulate wood, not generally a very satisfactory ploy since it betrays the excellent characteristics of both materials in the attempt to keep prices down. But it would be wrong to assume that only the expensive ranges are worth having. There are good buys at all levels, including kitchen units which are bought packaged flat and then assembled at home. However, when you have settled on your price level and are investigating what is available, watch for the following points:

1 If you are buying self-assembly units make sure the instructions are clear and full.
2 There should be a good, solid, wood carcass construction.
3 If the doors have wooden frames with clip-on laminated plastics panels, as several ranges do, be sure these are sturdy and stable. One particular range has panels which are so flimsy they can be easily pushed free at the corners. Small children would delight in pushing them to the limit and breaking them.

4 If you opt for wood-finished doors, choose a simple, elegant design rather than something so bedevilled with mouldings, flutings and foldings that it not only looks like something from a bygone age but will make your kitchen look dark and heavy, and be difficult to keep clean.
5 If the floor cupboards are not wall hung, choose a range where they stand on adjustable steel legs. This gives a small amount of height flexibility as well as coping with uneven floors.

1. Among the less expensive but beautifully designed Italian ranges, these units have laminated plastic-faced doors, and plastic work surfaces with curving, post-formed front edges. Décor panels hide refrigerators and dishwashers, and there are small, unobtrusive metal handles. 2. One of the best British ranges uses wood with great simplicity but to good effect. The wood is natural oak, the handles are flush brass rings, and floor-standing units have adjustable metal legs behind their plinth panels, which are faced in laminated wood veneer for hard wear. This picture shows a laminated plastic work surface, and there are lighting shields beneath all wall cupboards. 3. Designer Andrew Holmes retained the existing dresser and cupboards when he fitted out his kitchen. He painted them bright green, and constructed a simple plywood work surface which is supported on gas-barrel legs (linked by Klee Klamps). This he faced with white tiles, and inset gas hobs and a splendid custom-made stainless steel sink and drainer.

6 Look at the handles. The best are simple wooden knobs, flush brass rings, extruded aluminium tracks or wooden recessed channels. Avoid anything flimsy, bulky, aggressively shaped or difficult to clean, for handles are simply functional objects to open the drawers and doors, and should not be dominant features designed to catch your eye – or fall off after six months.

7 Think of cleaning and wear. Wood should have been treated with a plastic lacquer so that it can be easily wiped, laminated plastics finishes should be of good quality so that they do not easily chip or scratch. Plinths are best painted black or metal faced, so that they do not suffer from kick marks.

8 Interiors. These too should have easily cleanable surfaces (laminated plastics or lacquered wood are good), adjustable shelves and sturdy construction. Most ranges have a number of interior accessories – cutlery trays, deep wire baskets, swing-out storage shelves, racks for door backs, refuse bins, etc.

Examine your needs carefully before buying these. Attractive at first glance, they can be gimmicky, and they are a waste of money if never used.

9 Worktops. Most ranges have a variety of worktops to complement the cupboards. This may include ordinary square-edged laminated plastics, laminated plastics with a post-formed edge (the front edges and sometimes the back upstand are curved to give a softer line), waterproof groundwork to take tiles of your choice, or hardwood. There will be information on these surfaces later in the book (page 61). Suffice it to say here that each is perfectly satisfactory and much will depend on your personal predilection and your pocket, for they escalate in price roughly in the order I have arranged them.

Custom-made units

It is fairly rare now to find custom-made units in a new kitchen. The standard ranges, as I have described, are so varied, the permutations of finishes so large and the

1. Designer Jon Wealleans collects artefacts from the early years of this century – everything from chairs to fruit bowls – and has decorated his flat to match. Modern kitchen units would obviously not have fitted in, so he designed his own. They have grey laminated plastic surfaces and door fronts and grey-stained wooden frames. Asymmetrical handles evoke his chosen era – and are also perfectly functional. Note the old chimney opening which is now used as a cupboard with glasses ranged along the extended mantleshelf above.

2. There was something very attractive about the old-fashioned glass-doored kitchen cupboards, though you had to make sure the contents were tidy. This (rather expensive) Italian range has doors which are made of toughened checkerboard glass so that the contents are not on open view. There are hand-finished wooden frames, and modern refinements include contoured grooves for fingertip opening, strip lighting beneath wall cupboards and easy-to-clean laminated plastic work surfaces with a curved front edge.

3. This large kitchen/living room is used for many activities apart from cooking, and it was cleverly designed by its owner, Angela Chidgey, to present a very unkitcheny face to the world. Old pine cupboards, glass-fronted bookcases, chests of drawers and open shelves are all incorporated as storage at the kitchen end of the room which is shown here. Filled with their owner's collections of china, glass and straw baskets, they almost obliterate the room's true purpose and it comes as quite a surprise to see a brown enamel sink and cooker and dishwasher set unobtrusively into this homely arrangement. A plastic-faced cork floor – eminently suitable for the kitchen but with a soft, warm appearance – contributes to the unworkmanlike charms of the room and also to the fact that despite its looks, it functions exceptionally well. This is a very large space but an equally satisfactory effect could be achieved in a small kitchen with, for instance, one chest of drawers and one glass-fronted cupboard.

quality so good (if you choose carefully) that most people are not prepared to go to the extra trouble of having furniture specially built; that is, unless a first-rate architect or designer is in charge who will produce something unique and beautiful for which the client is prepared to foot the bill, or unless the kitchen owner/planner is a DIY addict and fancies he can do a good cheap job himself.

In any case, all the attributes I have listed as being important for proprietary ranges will apply. Custom-made units work out better for an awkwardly-shaped kitchen where standard sizes do not fit in easily, and they might be better where the main user of the kitchen is either very tall or very short, so that a special height can be contrived for the work surfaces. And it will certainly mean that esoteric finishes and colours, or unusual combinations, not catered for by the manufacturers, can be used. There is also, certainly for some people, much satisfaction in having an interior which is quite unique, so that no one can walk in and say, 'Oh, I see

you've got so-and-so's units.' And there is absolutely no danger that such a kitchen will have the familiar look of a colour advertisement from a Sunday supplement.

Non-kitchen units

I shall describe the non-kitchen style under 'Decoration' (page 80). It is based on furniture originally intended for other purposes – washstands, wardrobes, chests of drawers, etc.

For sensible conversion into kitchen units, it should be of solid construction (even if shabby and currently in need of repair), and pieces which are going to range alongside one another should be of similar depth if any coherence is to be achieved. This does not necessarily apply to pieces which will be used in different areas or on different walls of the room. Similarly any item which is going to be used to support the work surface should be of an appropriate height (roughly 900 mm (3 ft) but variable according to the height of the main kitchen user). Width is the only dimension which is not of major importance, though obviously it should make sense in relation to the size of kitchen and to the other pieces of furniture you are going to use. Internal shelves should be of strong construction, and if they are flimsy or rickety, should be replaced. They will probably be made of wood which should be thoroughly cleaned and then treated with matt or glossy polyurethane lacquer so that they are easy to keep clean in the future. Besides cleaning, inspect all old furniture carefully for rot and beetle, and treat it with the appropriate curatives if necessary.

Ovens and hobs

These are described together because many people still prefer one free-standing cooker combining both funct-ions, rather than the fashionable separate hobs and oven. And of course, if you are in rented accommodat-ion or anywhere else where you do not intend to stay for a long time, it makes sense to put in a free-standing cooker you can take with you when you go; this is not so simple with the split-level, built-in variety.

The range is large. For a start you will decide between gas and electricity. Once, it was usual to advise that gas was the cheaper running option. It would be invidious to do so now, since *all* fuel costs are high and gas prices do not appear to be much lower than electricity. Gas was said, on the other hand, to be dirtier than electricity, though with a well-functioning extractor fan I have not personally found this to be true. Conversely, the disadvantages of electricity were said to be that ovens took longer to heat up, and hobs were less easily controlled. Now, there are ducted hot air systems in several makes of electric oven which mean they heat instantly and hobs are delicately controllable. Strikes? Either industry is susceptible. Design? Some good, much bad in both camps. It is really a question of personal preference, or of being forced to use electricity because there is no gas available, which does happen in some country districts. You can, if you are having built-in appliances, opt for a gas oven and electric hobs, or vice versa, or even for hobs working on both fuels, or for a cooker which has an electric oven and gas hobs.

Free-standing cookers can be very large, incorporat-ing double ovens, four hobs, a griddle and/or a grill, as well as a large storage drawer; or they can be very small with just a single oven. There is also a limited choice of very small cookers which stand on a work surface, and (apart from caravans) are really only suitable for bed-sits. Many of the free-standing cookers – even the smaller ones – are available with ceramic cooking hobs which are not as fiendishly expensive as when they first

Separating ovens and hobs means you can have different fuels for each, different manufacturers if you so desire, and easier planning options. In 1. there is an electric oven but gas-fired hobs, and the oven has been built into the space left by an old kitchen-range, with the hob set in a newly constructed run of work surface. 2. shows a large open studio with the kitchen arranged on one side of a central storage block – the oven built into the block, the hob in a projecting work surface which also houses the sink. 3. This is an extension to a country cottage and here the oven is built into what was the chimney flue and on the outer wall. The boiler is set into the same wall, and surrounding shelves both unify the arrangement, and, filled with books and ornaments, have a decorative quality of their own.

appeared on the market, some of the more expensive ones have the ducted hot air system already mentioned, and some have grills with a dual circuit so that only a part of the grill need be heated to cook a small amount of food. Most free-standing cookers made on the Continent have the grill incorporated into the top part of the oven, a point worth remembering when considering the purchase of such a model. For it has a definite effect on cooking methods, and recipes for such things as sponge cakes may have to be adapted accordingly. On the credit side, such cookers usually have a fold-down lid (there being no high-level grill) which makes an extra work surface when no cooking is taking place on the hobs.

The built-in fittings are infinitely variable. The main components are: gas or electric ovens, either large or small, with or without grills; separate wall mounted grills, a very few of which are available for building-in; gas or electric hobs or a mixture of both fuels; electric ceramic hobs in black, white or brown; and something which was only at prototype stage at the time of writing but is probably now in full production, induction hobs which are activated simply by the touch of the pan on the

designated area (no control panels are necessary). In addition to all these things, there are some attractive ranges of separate hobs, deep-fryers, griddles and warm plates, any or all of which are intended to be set directly into the work surface.

There is no doubt that if you are planning a kitchen for long-term use, this splitting of the oven and hobs does open up all sorts of interesting possibilities in the arrangements, as well as looking good.

Whether the appliances are free-standing or built in, looks and function are equally important, and it is a pity that too many pieces of equipment, whilst being satisfactory overall in both respects, fail dismally on the details.

The general shapes, sizes and technical specifications are fine. So are the minor innovations like tinted glass doors, stay-clean oven linings, interchangeable door hinging and automatically controlled hobs which you can safely leave to simmer your stew. However, when it comes to design details, things are not so good. Watch out for an excess of poor-quality chrome trimmings. These are not only quite hard work to keep gleaming and smear-free, they are also likely to loosen

and come away in your hand after hard use.

Watch out for *anything* which is difficult to clean, such as poorly designed hobs (the gas industry is particularly culpable in this respect), awkward knobs with dirt-attracting crevices around and beneath them, and oven doors with long slim handles which fit so close to the door you cannot clean beneath them.

Some materials are more easily cleaned than others too. Chrome, as I have indicated, needs constant attention, and stainless steel despite its name is rather in the same category, so remember this when looking at cookers with admittedly handsome stainless steel doors. One particular manufacturer has rings on his gas hobs made of a nameless metal alloy which is the very devil to detach from its dirt. Enamel, on the other hand, whether on door surfaces or hobs, or coating gas rings, is easily wiped clean – and incidentally is available in a limited but pleasant range of colours.

Do not, then, be beguiled by a flashy appearance, even if you have flashy tastes. You will find it difficult to maintain. Go for discreet simplicity, where the controls are easily grasped and easily cleaned, the graphics clear (some, in an effort to be trendy, are aping computer graphics with grotesque and illegible results) and the colours pleasant and harmonious with everything else in your kitchen.

This is the place to mention the microwave cooker, although it is not something every household will want.

A microwave cooker is powered by electromagnetic short-length, high-frequency radio waves which cook food both inside and out simultaneously and thus more quickly. A 50 to 75 per-cent time saving is claimed by manufacturers, with the resultant saving in electricity and therefore money.

The microwave oven is used for cooking frozen food, for reheating cooked meals, and for straightforward oven cooking. However, the food emerges rather pallid and unappetizing-looking, and in need of a quick browning under the grill. Some microwaves have their own browning element built in, and at least one forms part of a triple oven complex (the other two being straightforward electric ovens).

4

1. A built-in combination microwave and normal oven with special circulating hot air system for rapid, even flow of heat. Both ovens have left- or right-opening doors, clear control panels and no crevices. 2. This ceramic hob fits neatly into a work surface. The hob indication light remains after switch-off until the heated area is safe to touch. Low simmer settings are possible and a white version is available. 3. Hob units line up and match perfectly but can be individually bought. Shown here are a deep fryer, electric hot plates, a single electric plate and a heat-resistant steel parking surface. Gas units and warming plates, sink units and ceramic hobs are also available. 4. A built-in double oven with electronic oven timer and digital clock. The top oven has a built-in spit and a grill which can be used half-on for economy, while the bottom oven has a constantly circulating hot air system. 5. A mixed-energy hob with an enamelled surface, available in red, green and bronze as well as white (a matching oven is available in the same colours). 6. The free-standing cooker *par excellence*. With double gas ovens, four gas hobs and a grill which is raised and lowered by a motor control, it also has a storage drawer at the base. A really good-looking British design.

5

6

The microwave oven seems to me a good extra buy for those who use a lot of frozen food (commercial or home-prepared), or who live in a bed-sit or caravan, because it does not get so hot and there are few cooking smells. It is not essential in most family kitchens.

Sinks

The next most important piece of equipment in your kitchen, like it or not, is the sink. I sometimes think we Brits would have gone on slogging away at our anonymous-looking stainless steel models for ever. But fortunately, Continental manufacturers were more inspired than our own, and thanks to their lead the options have increased considerably.

There is, of course, nothing wrong with stainless steel *per se* (though unless like a friend of mine you are prepared to care for it and buff it up with a soft cloth after every use, it soon loses its initial glitter), and there are innumerable sinks in this material on the market. There are twin sinks of equal size with or without integral drainers, twin sinks where one is larger than the other and where the smaller sink can be equipped with a waste-disposal unit and kept mainly for this purpose (satisfactory where there is a dishwasher), twin sinks separated by a small sink which again can be fitted with a waste-disposal unit but where there is no dishwasher so that two large sinks are necessary, and twin sinks of various shapes and sizes, not linked and not having drainers but which can be dropped individually into the work surface.

Stainless steel is a hygienic material, easy to clean even though its gleaming surface does become dimmed over the years by a myriad of tiny scratches. Those who like colour, though, will appreciate the enamelled steel sinks emanating from the Continent. The permutations are as varied as those for stainless steel, the colours of some makes are good, and there is much emphasis on accessories and fittings like plastic draining-baskets and sieves. These mean you really get value out of the space taken up by the sink or sinks. Many are circular, which look attractive, but be sure not to purchase one which is too small to be useful at all times.

That brings me to the question of sizes generally. The main (or only) sink should be at least 500 × 350 mm (20 × 14 in) if it is to take the largest item most people wash, which is an oven shelf – and this unfortunately precludes most of the circular sinks. Depth should be 175 – 200 mm (7 – 8 in) but 250 mm (10 in) if you are going to use the sink for hand laundry. Double sinks should have at least one of this maximum size, but the other could be smaller, say 350 × 250 mm (14 × 10 in), to be used for waste disposal, vegetable washing, etc.

China sinks, along with other items of a simple, back-to-the-farmhouse nature have enjoyed a revival in recent years. I do not think they are ideal for general kitchen use, since with heavy wear they will crack and chip, making them unhygienic as well as unsightly. But if you have a laundry room or large separate laundry area, they are excellent for hand-washing of clothes; many stainless steel or enamelled sinks are not really capacious enough for this purpose.

The way in which modern sinks can be set into the work surface varies. They may have their own integral drainer or drainers which do restrict the usage of the whole area to this one purpose. Or the sinks can be let directly into the work top with no drainers. If you have a dishwasher and are prepared to drain pans and other items you have washed by hand in the second sink, this

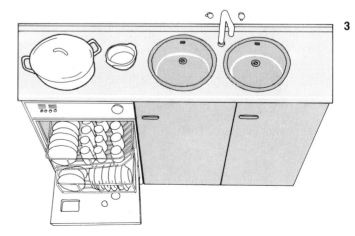

arrangement works. It looks neat and more precious worktop space is released for general use. The joint between worktop and sink must be good and tight though, or water will seep into it. Drainers are also designed now to be inset in the same way as sinks, which is another good-looking and practical innovation.

Kitchen sinks are now usually either stainless steel or enamel, and the latter allows more opportunity for colour. 1. is a single sink with integral drainer all in stainless steel. To be set on top of the work surface, it does not have the elegant simplicity of some custom-made models. 2. These inset circular sinks and drainers have a tough enamelled surface in shaded blue. Eleven other colours are available, but the 390 mm interior diameter would make this sink too small for some purposes. 3. Twin circular sinks set into the work surface, with a dishwasher close by so no need for special drainers – the small amount of draining necessary can take place in one sink. 4. A simple, deep stainless steel sink 483 mm diameter, which would meet most needs. 5. Two circular sinks fitted with cutting board and a drainage basket infinitely extend the use which can be given to the sink space.

4

5

Dishwashers

If there are more than two in the family, if at least two meals a day are eaten at home and/or if you entertain frequently, then a dishwasher would be a considerable asset in your kitchen. It would save time, energy and possibly even the china, since a dishwasher will not have the mishaps to which human hands are prone.

The criteria when judging which make and model you want are: capacity, performance and looks.

Exterior size is generally 600 mm (2 ft) width, 600 mm (2 ft) depth and 820–850 mm (2 ft 9 in) height. Maximum capacity is for fourteen place-settings, though the average washer holds twelve settings, and of course, there is no need to fill up in one go. Dishes can be fed in over the course of a day and then dealt with in one large evening wash. However, even on this basis a small family would have difficulty satisfying such a ravenous appetite for dirty dishes and there are certainly machines with a smaller capacity. The smallest take about three table-settings. Unlike the large machines which normally fit under a work surface or are built in at a higher level, and which are usually plumbed in to the water supply, these sit on top of the work surface and can have a simple hose connection (though they can be plumbed in if required). Suitable for an elderly couple or person living alone, these smaller machines are pleasant luxuries, though anyone with a quick or impatient temperament would probably rather wash the relatively few dishes involved by hand.

Performance of many of the machines is sophisticated – in some cases ludicrously so, for I cannot think it is necessary to have the thirteen programmes claimed by at least one manufacturer. Such *embarras de richesses*! But it is certainly important to choose a machine which copes with pans, which has a programme to cope with lightly soiled dishes as well as the real dirties, and one which has been insulated to make it quieter (some older models are bad in this respect). If you live in a hard water area choose a model with an integral water softener.

Not surprisingly the ubiquitous microchip has found its way into some dishwashers. Its principal advantage is that a larger number of functions and options can be housed in its tiny control package, with sophisticated

1

programming helping to save electricity.

When it comes to appearance, dishwashers are reasonably designed, though some control panels are inevitably more streamlined and simpler to understand than others. Some have neater graphics and some are in pleasant, appropriate colours, whilst others are crude and brash. I particularly object to the machine whose plastic switches are in two shades of mauve though this is, I admit, a subjective approach. White doors are white doors, but apparently offensive to some, so many machines have an optional décor frame into which a panel may be fitted to match your kitchen – or even to contrast with it. And some unit manufacturers offer separate doors behind which your dishwasher (and washing machine) may be completely concealed.

Washing machines

Washing machines have always seemed to me the best aid of all, and essential in the modern kitchen or laundry room. Even one person generates a huge amount of

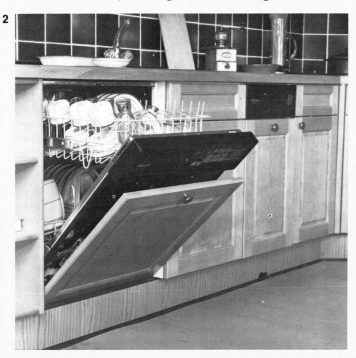

1. The dishwasher (right) holds twelve place-settings, and has a useful self-cleaning filter and comprehensible control panel. The washing machine (left), from the same manufacturer, has ten wash programmes, including an economy wash which saves 50% power and copes with 4.5 kg (10 lb) of washing – slightly more than average. These two models are available in red, almond and copper colour as well as white.

2. This seven-programme dishwasher may be concealed behind a door which matches the kitchen units sold by the same manufacturer. Only the control panel reveals its utilitarian presence.

washing in a week (think of sheets, tea towels, towels, underwear, shirts, jeans, table linen). Unless you relish the idea of a convivial hour at the launderette, a hard morning at the sink or a huge bill from the laundry, you will want a washing machine.

Twin-tub washers which are not fully automatic and where you must transfer the wash from one tub to another for spin-drying are still available. They are cheaper than a fully automatic machine and have a shorter wash cycle. But they take up a good deal of space and seem to me incomparably less desirable than a fully automatic machine.

The latter can be plumbed in to the hot and cold water system, or attached manually if more convenient. They can be top or front loading, and the latter are usually in standard exterior sizes to fit below or flush with kitchen work surfaces, coping with loads of 4–5 kg (9–11 lb). There are such variations in shape as a very narrow tall model which might solve some space problems, and a compact model which is about half the size of normal automatics in every dimension – including performance time.

As with dishwashers, washing machines come with a variety of programmes – one has twenty-two! – to cope with different types of wash. But again I think they have been overdone and that the absolute maximum requirement is the nine programmes suggested by the International Textile Care Labelling. Other programmes will probably never be used, so why pay for them?

Micro-electronic washing machines are in their early stages and developments, as in other branches of the chip business, will probably be rapid. Time, temperature and agitation are precisely controlled in this type of machine, faults are self-diagnosed and there is a resultant saving in time and money.

Some washing machines have integral tumble-driers which, although expensive in terms of electricity consumption, are invaluable for those with no indoor or outdoor drying facilities, as well as for those who are unable (by reason of ill health or even idleness) to pin up clothes on a line. Many have a reverse action which removes creases to the extent that some fabrics, such as cotton polyester, need virtually no ironing. The best also have a condenser which consumes the steam generated, so that the machine does not need to be vented to the outside world.

Separate tumble-driers are also available, many matched with washing machines of the same make so that they can be ranged alongside or stacked on top of them. Some of these have integral condensers and some can be programmed to take your washing to the exact stage of dampness required.

Whilst we're in the washing department, separate spin-driers are available for those who must do their washing by hand and want some assistance with the wringing-out. They do seem an anachronism – almost as archaic as mangles – and I think it is worth moving heaven and earth and every cupboard in the place if necessary to make room for an automatic washing machine.

Design of control panels is good on the whole, but if you are choosing a model with one of the extensive programme lists I have mentioned, make sure the graphics and switching instructions are perfectly explicit.

Refrigerators and freezers

These are lumped together, though I consider the former an essential and the latter an optional extra. Even in our relatively cool climate, you can keep food safe to eat and more attractive for a longer period with the aid of a refrigerator. It need not be large and requirements will, as with everything else, vary with the size and habits of the household. Refrigerators are available to slide under work surfaces, to sit on top of work surfaces, to be free standing or to be completely built into a range of kitchen

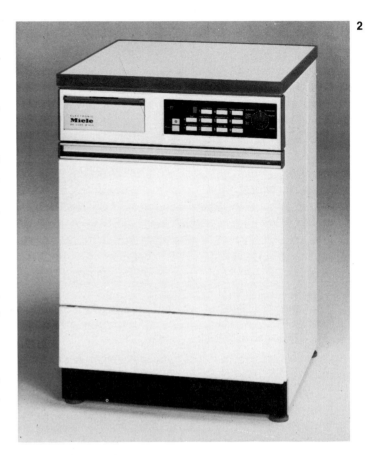

4

5

1. The British manufacturers of this microprocessor-controlled washing machine claim that it is the most sophisticated in the world. There is certainly precise control over such variables as time, temperature and agitation, and if ever it goes wrong, this machine is capable of self-diagnosis. There are various 'modification buttons' – spin-hold or extra wash, for instance – and if certain modifications cannot be used with the selected programme, the machine will indicate the fact. Fools are suffered gladly. This seems like the real beginning of the technological revolution in the kitchen.

2. Another electronic washing machine has an exceptionally well-designed control panel and a wide selection of programmes.

3. Designer John Dievel built a large cupboard to house his refrigerator; fitted with shelves on both the walls and the inner side of the door, it doubles as a larder.

4. Some manufacturers are producing their kitchen equipment in colour. This fridge/freezer, coloured bright red, presents a much less obtrusive and glacial face to the world than it would if it were the more traditional white. The same manufacturer produces dishwashers, washing machines, cookers and hobs in colours which include green and gold as well as red.

5. A specially made wooden unit designed and built to the exact dimensions of the fridge that hides behind it.

units within a housing frame. And décor frames are available with a number of models. Whatever your esoteric requirement, a diligent plod around the electricity showrooms is likely to reveal it. Gas refrigerators are also available, but the range is fairly limited and may not produce one to suit your needs.

Many models have doors which can be hinged on either side and this could be an important factor in a tightly planned kitchen. Some have automatic defrosting with evaporation of the defrost water – a marvellous innovation for those like me who have chipped away with knives, pans of hot water and the floor inches deep in water over the years.

Most refrigerators have a deep-freeze compartment with star markings to show the number of weeks it is safe to keep frozen food in it. For many families, a large compartment of this sort will serve their needs adequately, taking a loaf of bread and a few packets of ready-frozen vegetables and meat.

There are, however, others for whom a freezer really is a considerable benefit. These will include keen cooks who like to collect a stock of prepared meals, gardeners who have a plenitude of produce to hoard away, the overworked who can only spare one afternoon every

two months for a huge shopping expedition, those who live far from town . . . For such as these a freezer is more than a luxury, and they can choose between an upright model which uses little floor space and is easy to keep tidy and well organized, a combination fridge/freezer, which is similar but with the freezer ranged alongside or above a refrigerator, or a chest shape which is good for housing great joints of meat but takes up considerable floor space and is often better housed in the garage, laundry room or cellar than in the kitchen.

Do not overestimate your needs, like the lady for whom an architect struggled to fit a huge freezer into the new kitchen. When he did his six-months' inspection of the house, he opened the lid of the freezer to discover two packets of frozen peas in one corner – a waste of space and money, not to mention energy. Capacities range from about 50 litres (11 gallons) for models to stand on a work surface to over 600 litres (130 gallons) which would be a large chest.

Waste-disposal units

As a keen advocate of the waste-disposal unit, I have been regarded with horror by gardeners: 'But you can't chuck all your waste down the sink – what about the compost heap?' As a keen gardener, I agree with them. But if you live in a flat without an easily accessible garden, or if you have no garden, or if you do not love your garden, or if you are frantically trying to throw together a large meal at high speed, well then a waste-disposal unit set into one sink (you really do need to have a disposal unit set into a separate sink) will save you endless wrapping-up of peelings, scraps and small bones for depositing in the dustbin. This leaves you with tins, bottles and other hard stuff. Even that can be dealt with by a compactor – a machine which compresses such matter (deodorizing it *en passant*) into packages about one-fifth of the original size. Expensive but covetable, compactors are housed in small cabinets designed to fit under the work surface.

Extractor fans

A vitally important kitchen aid is the extractor fan which will remove food smells, steam, and perhaps most important, help to prevent condensation.

This can take the form of a relatively inexpensive fan unit set into a window or outside wall, but far more efficient is the built-in extractor unit comprising fan and hood which can be set above the cooker or, best of all, concealed in a cupboard unit over the cooker. Ducts will take all fumes away to the outside, but if for some reason ducting is not possible, a fan unit fitted with carbon filters can be used and in this case the air is recirculated with most of the fumes being extracted as they pass over the carbon filters – not so good but infinitely better than nothing.

Taps

There are sadly few good-looking taps on the market, that is unless you like shapeless and slippery blobs of acrylic for handles, faceted and complicated shapes and a general absence of thought or reason in the design. Taps are also shown in the bathroom section of the book, but of the very few sensibly designed ones, those suitable for kitchens – which includes swivel mixers to use with double sinks – are shown here. Incomparably the most handsome are the range

3

1. **A simple, specially made zinc hood gathers up all fumes from this gas hob and they are then whisked away by an extractor fan. Note also the neat detailing of the marble surface and upstand, and the inset stainless steel sinks with draining in wooden racks above. This kitchen was designed by John McConnell for his own home.**

2. **Plastic-topped taps worked by a simple lever action. This mixer tap is in white, but there are bright-red and deep-blue versions. Single taps and shower fittings are included in the range.**

3. **Excellent brass copies of old-fashioned cross-head taps come in two sizes, the larger suitable for the bath or the kitchen sink, the smaller suitable for a wash bowl.**

2

designed by Danish architect Arne Jacobsen, and as well as being sold in polished brass or with a chrome finish, they are also available in a marvellous range of colours, around one of which you could build a whole kitchen. But they are expensive. At the other end of the scale are two good ranges of plastic taps. It is a pity that one of these has been modified and marred since it won a Design Council award several years ago, but the design is still better than most.

I have always liked the old-fashioned cross-head taps and apparently lots of other people do too because some rather second-rate modern copies are selling well. Very beautiful and exact reproductions of these taps are also on the market (see the bathroom section, page 88) but they are expensive.

1. Danish-designed mixer tap is shown here with a red epoxy finish, but several other colours are available, as well as chrome and polished brass. Wall-mounted spouts, stand-up taps, shower outlets and various other arrangements are all included in this modern range for either kitchen or bathroom use. 2. An Italian version of the old cross-head style tap is epoxy resin coated in various colours. Shown here is the sink mixer in green.

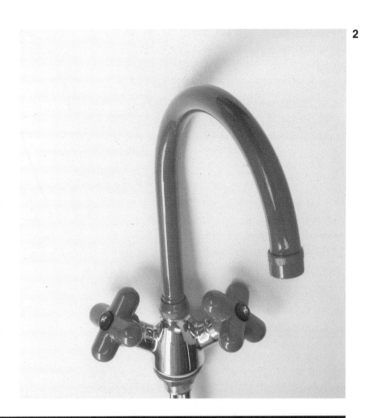

Planning

Whether you are shuffling around a few battered units from an existing kitchen and reviving them with some carefully chosen pieces of new equipment, or whether you are lucky enough to be building the whole thing new, there are some basic principles you should try to apply to the project. These are not rules. If you find one of them impossible to incorporate into your particular set-up, do not assume that all is lost. It is surprising what you can get used to, and I have seen some most successful and attractive kitchens which flout a great many of the rules. Also, you may have acquired a few habits over a lifetime of cooking which are going to need strenuous efforts to break. Don't try. Plan your kitchen around the way *you* like to work, incorporating as many of the principles as you find yourself warming to.

Here they are:

1 For real economy in the construction or alteration work, site the sinks and dishwasher as near to the existing plumbing as possible. And to avoid lengths of expensive ducting from the extractor fan, place the hobs and oven on an outside wall.

2 Whatever the shape of your kitchen, try to have the sinks, oven and hobs set in a continuous run of work surface, with no gaps or obstacles such as tall fittings

between. This sequence, known as Parker Morris after the author of the report in which it was first recommended, does not have to be in a straight line. It can for instance, be down two adjoining walls, or down three, in a U-shape.

3 Going on from this, make a short work triangle composed of cooker, sinks and refrigerator, with the total distances of the triangle sides (however large the kitchen) being between 3.6 m (12 ft) and 6.6 m (28 ft). This triangle should be off the main circulation route to avoid accidents.

4 Aim to have storage cupboards near to where the equipment they house will be used, i.e. saucepans storage near the cooker, china storage near sink and dishwasher, etc.

5 Try to have the larder on an east- or north-facing wall.

This drawing shows the classic Parker Morris work sequence, with cooker, sink and hob set in a continuous run of work surface (in this case U-shaped) with no gaps or obstructions. Note the ample areas of work surface and the adjacent cupboards for storing ancillary equipment.

However small, large, or otherwise inconvenient the kitchen you are planning, you will with careful forethought probably be able to incorporate most of these principles; though 'careful forethought' may in this case mean employing an architect or designer to do the job for or with you. Choose him or her carefully (see the Introduction).

Assuming that you are going to do your own planning, most pundits recommend that you should take a sheet of squared paper, measure your kitchen and then reproduce its scaled-down shape on this paper, adding the measured shapes of all the fittings and equipment you want to fit in. Fine, if you are not a halfwit about measured drawings. I fear I am. So I use a much simpler method involving coloured chalk and a steel tape, in the room involved. Do persevere with the pencil and paper though, as it is really far more satisfactory.

With the major principles incorporated, the following points are also worth bearing in mind:

1 Much time is spent at the sink, even when there is both a dishwasher and washing machine, so it is pleasant to have the sink set under a window – unless the view is of a blank wall, dustbin area or somewhere equally unpleasant.
2 Take care that doors, both in the walls and to fitted cupboards and equipment, open in the right direction. The right direction can be either to the right or to the left, but it should ensure that there is no obstruction caused by barring a narrow passageway or by clashing with another door opening nearby.
3 Avoid wall storage over cookers. The dangers are obvious and the effects of steam and cooking fumes can be destructive. An extractor hood concealed within a cabinet (as mentioned on page 52) is another matter.

4 If possible have a separate area or even room for laundering clothes. Dirty linen and fresh food are not really ideal stablemates. Nor are clean linen and cooking smells. If there is a large bathroom this would be a much more appropriate place to site laundry equipment. If it must be in the kitchen, a separate sink area is ideal. In a small kitchen, try to keep the washing machine away from the refrigerator, larder and food preparation area.

Measurements

You will note I have not gone into excessive detail about ideal measurements in front of and between appliances. These, though constantly cited, seem the source of much needless aggravation. Common sense is more important than worrying about the number of millimetres between your open oven and the nearest stretch of work surface.

There is one measurement, however, that is of vital importance, and that is height of work surface.

Height of work surface
Research at Loughborough University has shown that no single working top height is best for all users. Well, I could have told them that. Nor, it seems, is one height level suitable for all activities. Again, they have reached

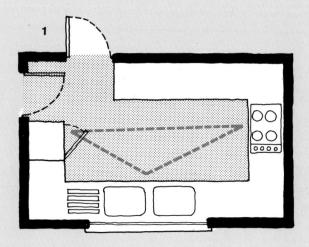

an obvious conclusion. But what can we do? We grow to different heights, we perform various activities in our kitchens, but most proprietary cupboard units are, not surprisingly, made to a standard height. The British Standard metric height which is generally adopted for work surfaces and sink rims is 900 mm (36 in), but if the main kitchen user is either very short or very tall, this will prove uncomfortable – try cutting a loaf of bread at this height if you are only five feet tall.

1. This shows the work triangle composed of cooker, sinks and refrigerator; it is off the main circulation route.

2. Crockery storage is easily accessible to both sink and dishwasher in this small kitchen, with low-level cupboards, shown 3., for storage of pots and pans adjacent to the oven and built-in ceramic hob.

4. All equipment – oven, hobs, refrigerator/freezer and dishwasher are built in to this carefully planned kitchen which has a separate laundry area beyond. There is a foldaway extractor hood over the hob, and the sink is sensibly set under the window, with the dishwasher close by.

5. Again there is an extractor hood set over the cooking hobs, but as it was vital to cut costs, this was set as close to the outside wall as possible. Trunking, concealed within high-level cupboards, quickly and inexpensively transports cooking fumes to the exterior. A hood is not absolutely essential. Fairly satisfactory results can be achieved if a powerful fan is set directly into an outside wall above the cooker.

If you are having custom-built units it is fairly easy to arrange the height you want. Standard units create more problems, although plinths can be reduced by 50–80 mm (2–3 in), or conversely, increased. And some of the best-quality floor units are mounted on adjustable steel legs behind their plinths which give a very small variation. And of course, the short wall-hung unit is easily adjustable. Be warned though, that if the work surfaces are too low they will not accomodate built-in appliances designed to fit under standard height surfaces.

That is not the end of the matter, however. The Loughborough research indicated that in an ideal kitchen, the sinks and draining boards should be about 75 mm (3 in) higher than the normal work surface to allow for reaching down into the sink. Since this would involve a change of levels in the work surface, I would personally rather forgo it. You may feel differently – in which case ensure that the change comes in a safe position, and not, for instance, close to the cooker hob or interrupting a long unbroken stretch of work surface.

Storage

The planning of storage is a greatly overworked subject. Unit manufacturers have a vested and understandable interest in encouraging us to buy as many cupboards as possible, hence the plethora of cupboards, floor to ceiling, which line the walls of many an overdesigned kitchen. Be bold and open the odd door or two in such a kitchen, and within you will often find the most almighty collection of unused and forgotten junk. Or you might find nothing. Do not be caught in the manufacturers' trap. Divide the kitchen into storage groups and work out what you need for each, as follows:

Larder

Many modern houses do not have them. In fact my husband, in his younger-days, designed me a kitchen without one and I was foolish and inexperienced enough to allow him. The mistake has never been repeated.

A ventilated larder, preferably on the north or east wall

1. In this conservatory/kitchen which architect John Thompson designed as an extension to his own house, the main cooking and serving area is cleverly separated from the clothes-washing area by a projecting peninsula unit. 2. shows the other side of this peninsula where the washing machine and tumble-drier are tucked away. Because this surface is slightly higher than others in the kitchen it forms a visual as well as a physical barrier.

3. To double the use of the space beneath the sink, the owners of this kitchen have made a pull-down front on the back of which there is a broad shelf to house all the bottles and canisters used at the sink.

and with deep, wipe-clean shelves, is the very best place for storing vegetables, fresh fruit, cooked meat and dry-store foods such as flour, sugar, dried fruits, biscuit tins – and in fact virtually every foodstuff which is not kept in the refrigerator or freezer. It should be situated as near as possible to the food preparation area.

Wet cleaning materials

Every kitchen will have its quota of liquid soap, bleach, pot scourers, soap, scrubbing brushes, buckets and the like. They should be stored beneath the sinks, and since this space tends to be small, taken up by the undersides of the sinks and by waste disposal units, in the cupboards to either side. Do not allow any more cupboard space or you will find yourself hoarding half-used bars of soap, rotting dishcloths, clogged-up bottles of window cleaning liquid and other such unsavoury items, in an effort to justify its existence. The door back of one of these cupboards can have a frame to hold rubbish bags which are disposed of as filled. These seem the most hygienic refuse-disposal method;

or you can have a small bin inside one of the sink cupboards.

Dry cleaning items

A tall double cupboard will take brooms, mops and a vacuum cleaner, preferably clipped or hung on to the wall, with shelves above for polishes, dusters, brushes, dustpans and the like. This large cupboard need not necessarily be in the kitchen, for most of the things stored in it will be carried all over the house for use. So if kitchen space is limited, it can be on a landing, under the stairs or in a utility room. If it is in the kitchen it is best situated near the door leading to the rest of the house.

Ironing board

This too needs a tall cupboard and the temptation, not always resisted by me, is to keep it in the dry cleaning cupboard which is not clean enough. Best of all, it should let down from the wall and be housed in a slim cupboard of its own so that it can be used *in situ* and there is no heavy carrying involved. Some proprietary unit ranges have a cupboard for this purpose, and it can be situated in the kitchen, off the main circulation route, or better still in the laundry room, if you have one.

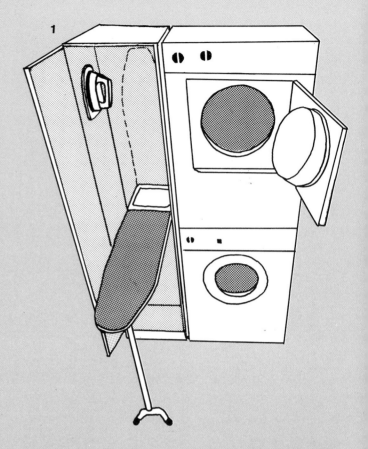

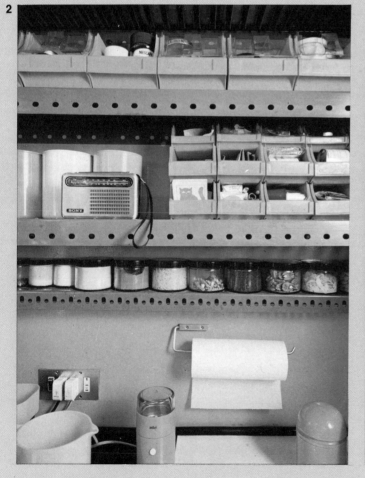

1. A let-down ironing board, housed in its own cupboard, complete with wall-mounted iron, makes ironing quicker and easier.

2. Good-looking jars, pots and other kitchen equipment can contribute to the decoration if they are carefully arranged – and kept that way. In Jan Kaplicki's kitchen, open industrial-type shelving is used and lots of red plastic storage bins.

3. An idea for a pull-out 'wall' for storing saucepans in the kitchen. Pan shapes are painted on the wooden wall to ensure that everything returns to its rightful place.

4. This kitchen has open shelves in wood, and to maximize a small space and lose a bad view they are taken right across the window.

5. A shallow drawer close to the cooker is the best place for storing all the small items – corkscrews, skewers, peelers, knives and so on – which are used in food preparation and which can easily be mislaid.

6. Wide vertical slots between cupboards are good for storing trays and hanging tea-towels, but must be wide enough to be easily cleaned.

Cooking utensils

These fall into two groups – those used in preparation and those used in the actual cooking.

Those used in cooking can be hung and stacked in one or two cupboards at low level near to the cooker, and will include saucepans, frying pans, heavy casseroles and baking tins. The preparation utensils tend to be lighter and can be stacked in one or two high-level cupboards above the work surface where most of the preparation will be done; bowls, measuring jugs, sieves, cooling racks and so on.

There should also be a shallow drawer beneath the work surface for small items such as potato peelers, skewers, pastry cutters and food trays, and a deep drawer for the bulkier items like rolling pins, whisks, food graters and strainers.

There are two schools of thought about storing kitchen knives. Personally, I like them safely stored away in a shallow drawer, but others are happy to have them in a wooden slot or magnetic strip fixed to the wall above the cooking surface. Ladles, fish slices and so on are certainly most accessible hung in this way. Other drawers in this area should include a deep one for all the appurtenances of a food mixer if you have one, another for rolls of greaseproof paper, tinfoil, clingfilm and plastic bags and string, and another for clean tea towels.

2

Eating equipment

When it comes to the items relating to the eating of food, i. e. crockery, cutlery and table linen, if food is eaten in the kitchen these should be stored midway between the sink (and/or dishwasher) and the table. They will probably require two high-level cupboards for china, a deep drawer for table linen and a shallow one for cutlery. If you have a dining room too, you will probably store some of the smarter china and cutlery and linen there. If not, double up on storage to accommodate it all in the kitchen.

Chopping boards and trays

These can be stored flat on a shelf below the preparation area, or even better, upright in a slot left between two cupboards. Tea towels in use can be hung on a pull-out rack fixed into a similar slot. Make sure this is wide enough for you to get your hand in to clean it.

More measurements

I am returning to this taxing and tedious subject for the sake of those who are not buying an expensive array of ready-made units which come in standard sizes, but who are adapting or building their own.

The standard base units are 600 mm (2 ft) wide (though these are variable in multiples of a hundred mm), 600 mm (2 ft) deep, with heights (including work surface) as given on page 37. Wall cupboards are again based on multiples of 600 mm (2 ft) wide but are only 300 mm (1 ft) in depth. This dimension is sufficient to accommodate large plates. When positioning the wall cupboards above the base cupboards, a gap of 400–450 mm (16–18 in) is generally recommended as

this will allow for the storage of small electrical equipment on the work surface and for bending over without bumping your head on the upper cupboards.

If you are building your own or cannibalizing old units or even converting somebody's handed-down sideboard into kitchen cupboards, try to keep as nearly as possible to these sizes. They were not plucked out of the air, but carefully worked out to suit most people's needs and body movements. And following on that, much kitchen equipment (dishwashers, cookers, etc.) is designed and sized to match. So the right measurements are worth struggling for in terms of comfort and convenience. Your kitchen will also have a more orderly and coherent appearance than one in which some cupboards jut out at one level, some at another, and where even the wall cupboards are at different heights.

If planning does not come easily to you and you are

1

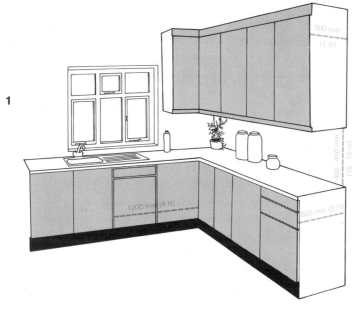

floundering hopelessly, look at some of the suggested layouts which follow at the end of this chapter. They are for both large kitchens and small, and they include very conventional shapes of the sort most of us have, and a couple which are both unusual and potentially awkward. You will not want to follow these plans down to the last broom cupboard, but they may release the log jam, start you thinking more freely, and provide at least a few ideas to help solve your own particular problems.

1. **When high-level cupboards are fixed above the work surface, be sure the gap between the two is sufficient to accommodate things like food mixers and coffee percolators which are likely to live there. A distance of 400–450 mm (16–18 in) should be enough for this and to prevent you banging your head every time you lean forward over the work surface.**

2. **This beautifully detailed and spacious kitchen/dining room has been well planned so that there are cupboards and drawers beneath the projecting eating bar on the left, and a bank of cupboards beneath the peninsula on the right, which houses the sink and which separates the main kitchen from the dining room. There is an upstand behind the sink which makes a good visual barrier between the two, and the wooden shelf running across the top makes a resting place for dishes, both full and empty, passing between the two sections of the room. This is a big room and everything is on a generous scale, but the same principles could be applied equally well to a tiny kitchen/dining room.**

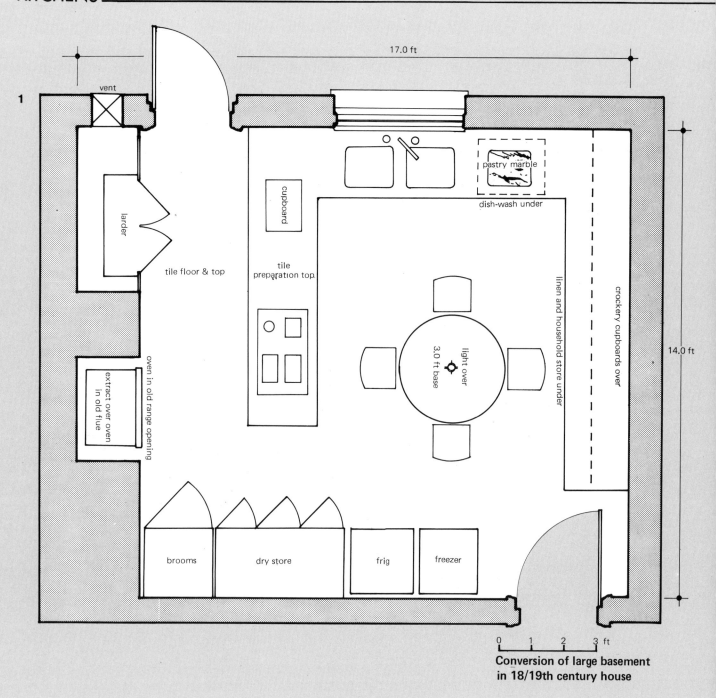

1

17.0 ft

vent

larder

tile floor & top

cupboard

tile preparation top

extract over oven in old flue

oven in old range opening

pastry marble

dish-wash under

linen and household store under

crockery cupboards over

light over
3.0 ft base

14.0 ft

brooms

dry store

frig

freezer

0　1　2　3 ft

**Conversion of large basement
in 18/19th century house**

Kitchens to eat in

There can be few families, however grand, who do not eat at least breakfast in the kitchen. Others eat most meals there, except when they have guests, and others have a dining kitchen as their only eating place.

Here are a few basic precepts for the planning of eating arrangements. The eating area can be treated in two ways. It can be separated off and used *only* for eating. Or it can be incorporated into the general design of the kitchen, with the table doubling up for other things when not in use. In this case the table can either be central and free-standing (in a large, square kitchen), or pushed against a wall, to be pulled out for eating, or

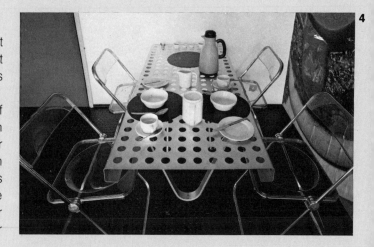

4

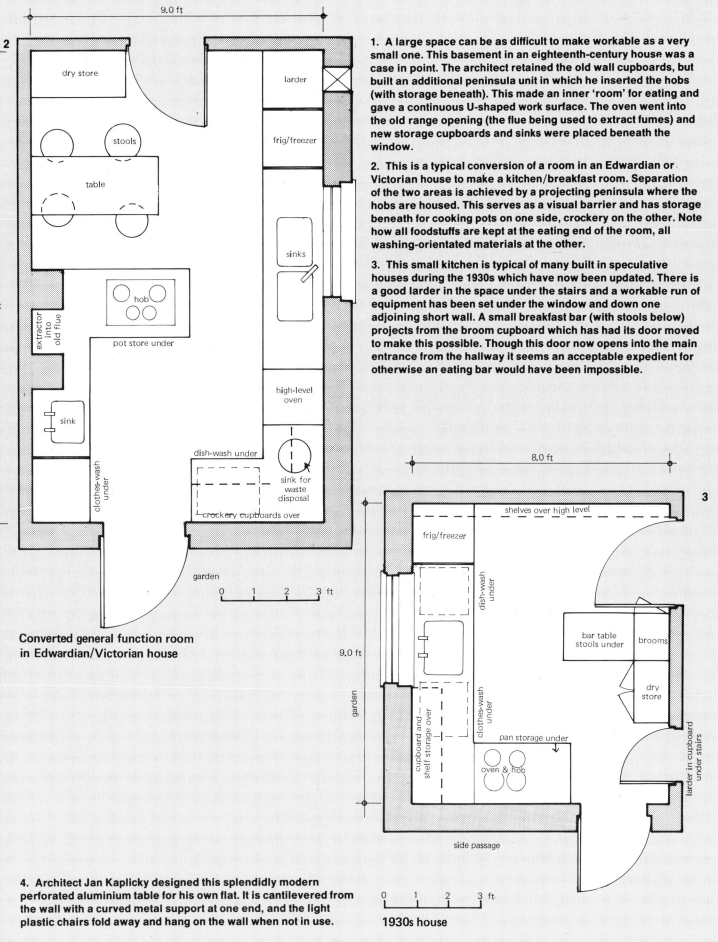

2

9.0 ft

dry store

stools

table

extractor into old flue

sink

clothes-wash under

hob

pot store under

larder

frig/freezer

sinks

high-level oven

dish-wash under

sink for waste disposal

crockery cupboards over

garden

0 1 2 3 ft

**Converted general function room
in Edwardian/Victorian house**

8.0 ft

3

shelves over high level

frig/freezer

dish-wash under

cupboard and shelf storage over

clothes-wash under

oven & hob

pan storage under

bar table stools under

brooms

dry store

larder in cupboard under stairs

9.0 ft

garden

side passage

0 1 2 3 ft

1930s house

1. **A large space can be as difficult to make workable as a very small one. This basement in an eighteenth-century house was a case in point. The architect retained the old wall cupboards, but built an additional peninsula unit in which he inserted the hobs (with storage beneath). This made an inner 'room' for eating and gave a continuous U-shaped work surface. The oven went into the old range opening (the flue being used to extract fumes) and new storage cupboards and sinks were placed beneath the window.**

2. **This is a typical conversion of a room in an Edwardian or Victorian house to make a kitchen/breakfast room. Separation of the two areas is achieved by a projecting peninsula where the hobs are housed. This serves as a visual barrier and has storage beneath for cooking pots on one side, crockery on the other. Note how all foodstuffs are kept at the eating end of the room, all washing-orientated materials at the other.**

3. **This small kitchen is typical of many built in speculative houses during the 1930s which have now been updated. There is a good larder in the space under the stairs and a workable run of equipment has been set under the window and down one adjoining short wall. A small breakfast bar (with stools below) projects from the broom cupboard which has had its door moved to make this possible. Though this door now opens into the main entrance from the hallway it seems an acceptable expedient for otherwise an eating bar would have been impossible.**

4. **Architect Jan Kaplicky designed this splendidly modern perforated aluminium table for his own flat. It is cantilevered from the wall with a curved metal support at one end, and the light plastic chairs fold away and hang on the wall when not in use.**

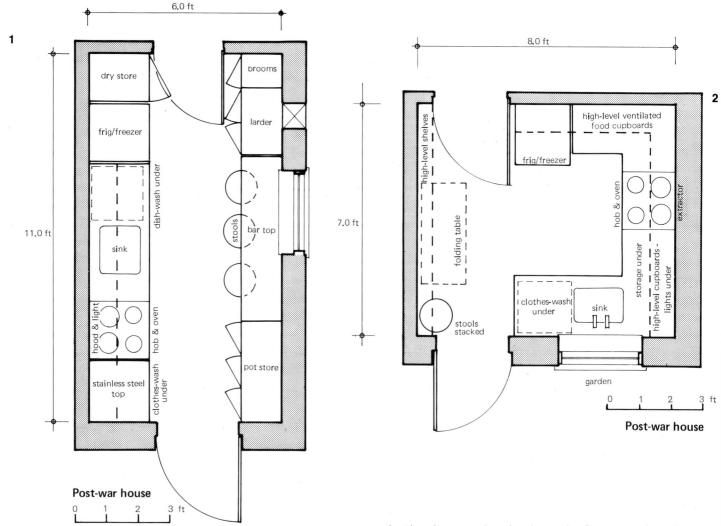

1. A galley kitchen with doors at both ends can be a problem, especially as it tends to act as a through-way. But in this post-war house, tight planning has made the best of things. All the working equipment – washing machine, cooker, sink, dishwasher and fridge/freezer – has been placed in a straight run down one side, while the other side is reserved for storage, with a narrow counter top inserted into it (and stools tucked away beneath) so that at least breakfast may be eaten here. This eating counter can also be used to augment the rather minimal area of work surface on the other side of the room.

2. This is another post-war house, but this time its small kitchen is virtually square. Because of the way the garden door is placed directly opposite the door into the hallway, this side of the kitchen becomes a corridor. All activities were therefore planned to take place out of this corridor, making a U-shaped work area. But a foldaway breakfast table can be erected just for mealtimes when – presumably – members of the family are not rushing from hallway to garden.

3. Not everyone lives in one huge open space. Artist Chloe Cheese does and she asked designer Andrew Holmes to design her an appropriate kitchen. Here, viewed from her gallery-bedroom, is the result. Sink, hotplate and oven are set into an island unit, with triangular-shaped work surfaces mounted on tubular legs and castors which can be pulled away and then joined up again to make a table when cooking is over and eating begins. Colours are brilliant red, blue and yellow. If your lifestyle includes a studio in a vast London warehouse, this witty kitchen design will be worth further consideration.

projecting in a peninsula shape in, for example, a long narrow kitchen.

It should preferably be well away from sink and cooker to avoid splashing, scalding or other unpleasantnesses for those sitting at it, but should, as described on page 42, have things such as cutlery, serving dishes and crockery stored nearby. Ideally, there should be an adjacent work surface to act as a serving space.

In the case of the completely separate eating area, the separation should be marked visually by something like a bank of waist-high cupboards which can act as both storage and as serving shelf; and it should, of course, be quite clear of the main access and circulation routes as well as the cooker and sink.

In either case, it would be good if space is available to have a worktop nearby to hold such small items as toasters, electric plate warmers and coffee percolators.

Even in a narrow galley kitchen or a tiny square one, it is generally possible to arrange a short section of work surface with knee room below, where two stools can be tucked away when not in use; and this makes a useful quick breakfast area for a small family or single people who are about to dash off to work.

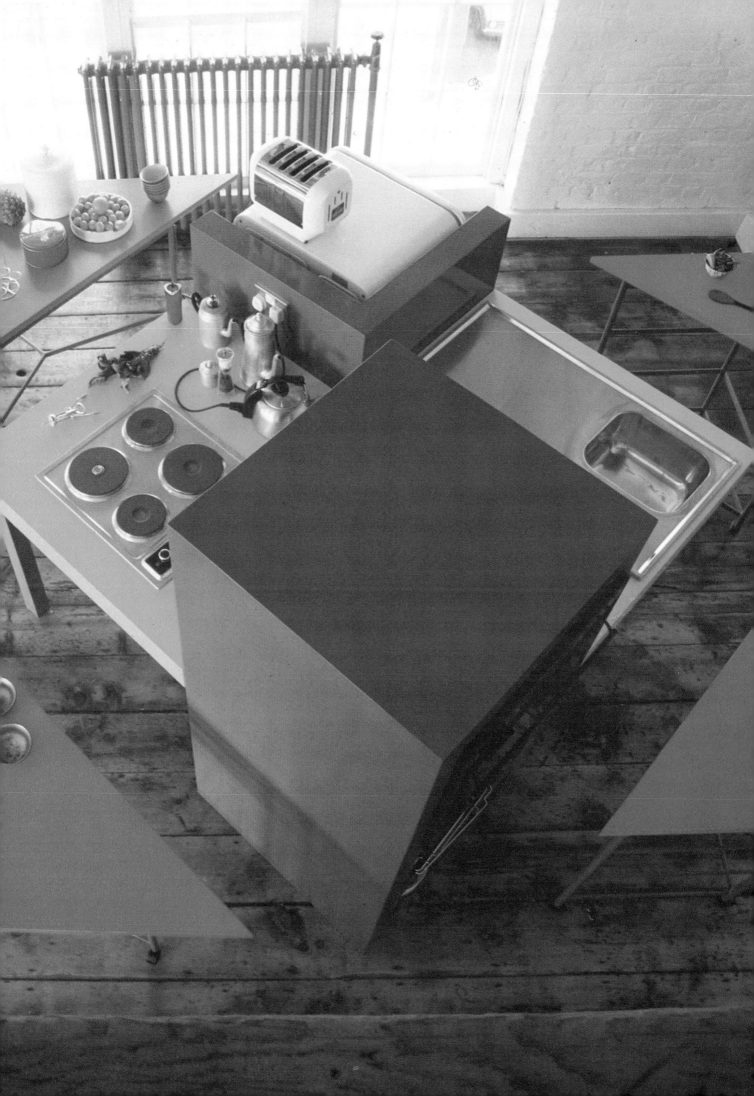

Technicalities

1. Designer John McConnell uses white-painted industrial light fittings over the equipment and work surfaces in his kitchen, with a low-hung ceiling pendant over the central table. 2. Tungsten spots are set into the ceiling and directed over the work surfaces. 3. In this high tech kitchen spots set into light tracks are fixed to proprietary-brand wire shelving, which is then suspended the length of the combined kitchen/dining room. 4. Fluorescent strip lighting with diffuser panel set into the ceiling. 5. Andrew Holmes designed this kitchen which has spots set into the ceiling; carefully directed spots light the dining end beyond the staircase. 6. Fluorescent lighting is concealed beneath the high-level cupboards.

However well laid out, furnished and decorated your kitchen is, unless the main services – lighting, heating, plumbing and fume extraction – work well, it is impossible to have everything running smoothly. If you are employing an architect or designer, his expertise should cover all aspects of this work. And even if you are your own planner, you will almost certainly be employing qualified tradesmen to do the actual installation work of a technical nature. All the same, you should be aware of the basic requirements and options open to you.

Lighting

Good lighting, both daylight and artificial, is essential in a kitchen if it is to be safe and comfortable. If the kitchen windows are not adequate to provide daylight, enlarge them, increase them in number or resign yourself to the use of a certain amount of artificial light during the day (this will often apply in basement kitchens). There is another alternative for a kitchen in a single-storey building (such as is often the case when the kitchen is an extension to an existing house). This is a roof light, and there are versions for both flat and pitched roofs. The quality of light from this type of overhead window is delightfully soft and clear, and the view of scudding clouds on the right sort of day equally good.

When it comes to artificial light, there should be a good overall level of illumination coupled with extra well-lit working surfaces, cooking hobs and oven. These standards are relatively easy to achieve by several different arrangements of light fittings. Examples are:

1 A pendant light over the central area and separate lighting for work surfaces.
2 Tungsten spots recessed into the ceiling for overall lighting, with a separate arrangement of wall-mounted spots strategically placed at a lower level to illuminate work surfaces, cooker, etc.
3 Track lighting set into the ceiling, parallel with and just in front of the work surfaces. The spots could be switched individually, so that those giving general illumination do not necessarily have to be on at the same time as those over the work areas.
4 Fluorescent tubes concealed behind wooden battens beneath high-level cupboards, or shelves over the work surfaces.

There are other types of lighting outlets, such as fluorescent strips set into the ceiling and diffused by glass panels, eyeball fittings which are only partly inset, and wall washers which are inset and can be arranged to give light on the area where it is required. But the two important points to consider are that you should have

7. Architect John Guest's house has a kitchen/living room at first-floor level; the whole working area of the kitchen is lit by very modern suspended light fittings.

8. Tony and Anne Barnes made this new kitchen out of a long narrow extension at the back of their house. To bring extra daylight they had this large rooflight built into the flat roof.

1

good overall lighting, and an extra high level of light over the working areas.

Heating – space and water

It is difficult to pontificate about heating the kitchen because so much depends on how the rest of the home is heated. Where there is general central heating by radiators or blown air, the kitchen will presumably be heated in the same way, the only decision being where best to site the radiators or warm air outlets. Radiators can be cumbersome appliances in any room, but remember they-are available in a variety of shapes – as skirting panels, as chunky,' attractively old-fashioned blocks, or as slim oblong panels – and can often be incorporated into the general arrangements in an ingenious and unexpected way. It is not uncommon, for instance, to see them mounted vertically instead of horizontally, which in a curious manner diminishes their presence; and the chunky radiators can fill a space at low level under something like an oven.

The boiler – oil, solid fuel or gas-fired – for the central heating can be sited in the kitchen, and some are small enough to fit neatly into a range of wall cupboards, though in·this case they must be very clean and well insulated. But a boiler of any considerable size is best concealed elsewhere; in a cellar, garage or asbestos-lined hall cupboard.

Water heating is generally linked to the central heating system where there is one, and in warm weather when the boiler is off this can be replaced by an electric immersion heater.

Where there is no central heating system, the kitchen must be heated independently, and it is important to ensure that the appliance used is both safe and convenient – definitely no open electric or gas fires in this busy and often watery setting. Gas or electric convector heaters, or infra-red heaters would all be satisfactory and they should all be wall mounted. A gas model would probably need a flue and have to be connected to an outside wall for this purpose, which might inhibit its use in a tightly planned room.

1. The breakfast bar in architect Pierre Botschi's kitchen is dramatically lit by three red pendant lights. 2. This basement kitchen sometimes needs artificial light during the day, so there are several ceiling-mounted tungsten lights, a pendant over the table and tube lights beneath high-level cupboards (not seen here). 3. A long radiator, mounted vertically, slightly recessed and painted the same cream colour as the wall, is relatively unobtrusive despite its size.

Water heating, in a non-centrally heated kitchen, is best achieved by an immersion heater which serves the whole house, or you may wish to have an instant heater, serving the kitchen alone and heating the water as and when it is needed. This might serve the purposes of a very small family who are out most of the time and do not have a dishwasher or washing machine.

Extraction

There are two major causes of condensation in the kitchen. One is cold surfaces, and the other is the action of steam on those cold surfaces. I've dealt with the question of keeping the room warm, so what about getting rid of all the steam generated by cooking and washing? An extractor fan is the answer, and as well as taking away steam it will do much to alleviate the greasy fumes which quickly build up a disgusting layer of dirt over everything if they are not tackled.

A simple fan model set in a window or wall is better than nothing, but a fan set into a cooker hood over the hob is the optimum arrangement. The hood gathers together all steam, smells and fumes which the fan then whisks away via a duct to the outside world. If the cooker is set against an outside wall, no expensive ducting will be necessary as the fan can be set directly into the wall, but in any case keep the ducting as short as possible for the maximum effect and conceal it within built-in cupboards or in the space above the false ceiling.

There are many proprietary hoods on the market, including some already set into cupboards which are part of standard ranges, but it is also possible to build in your own or even to have a fan over the cooker without the attendant hood, though inevitably this is not quite so effective.

If it is not possible to carry steam and fumes right away, which is sometimes the case when the cooker is located far from an external wall or if you are in rented accommodation and do not want to tamper with the fabric, there are cooker hoods which recirculate the air through charcoal filters. These filters remove smells and grease, so that you are not greeted by stale cooking fumes every time you enter the house, but do little to remove humidity. So you are still left with problems, and should certainly opt for the first (more expensive) type of hood if it is at all possible.

Plumbing

In a major conversion, or where an entirely new kitchen extension is being built, an architect will probably be involved to take care of this important matter. Or at least

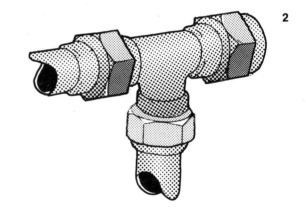

there will be a builder on the job who, it is hoped, employs a competent plumber.

If you are tackling the job yourself – and financial pressure is tempting some quite unlikely people into such bravery – do consult the local building inspector or district surveyor on this specific subject before you start.

Even if it is quite a small job you have in mind, such as moving the sink or repositioning a tap, talk to him first to avoid the sort of ghastly mistake easily made by an amateur. Beyond that, even if you have employed a plumber and are only acting as overseer, bear the following points in mind:

1 All water pipes should be easily accessible and not buried in solid walls or floors. On the other hand they should be concealed within cupboards, under shelves or above ceilings. That is, unless you like the look of plumbing pipes – unless, in fact, you are

3

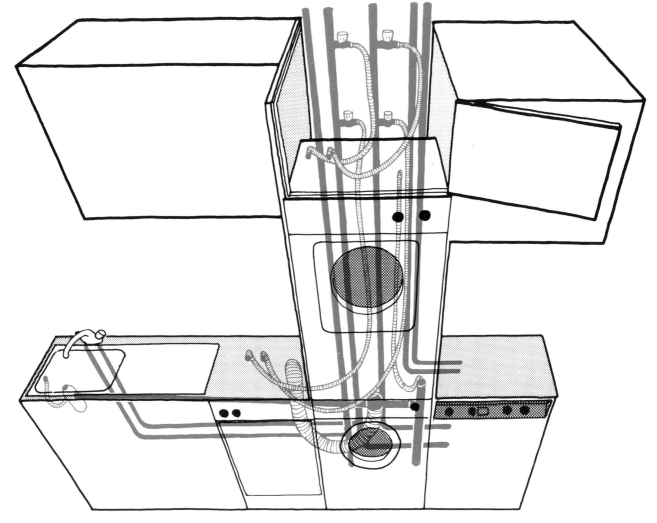

aiming for a sophisticated high tech look, where services are blatantly in the open. I warn you, it is something that only the most sophisticated and clever designer can normally bring off successfully, but more of that on page 70.

2 Drainage will normally consist of a 50 mm (2 in) waste pipe with a good gradient so there is no danger of small items of waste building up and causing a blockage. Have you ever banged away with one of those plungers in the exhausting effort to unblock a sink where this point has been overlooked? It is no fun.

3 All appliances will be connected to this waste, and there should be an access cap above each connection so that the pipe can be easily rodded through if a blockage *does* occur.

4 Be sure plastic pipes used for hot water are capable of withstanding high and fluctuating temperatures. Solid fuel boilers without thermostatic control, for instance, can cause trouble if the plastic pipes are not adequate.

5 Even if you are not at first installing all the appliances you plan to have, make sure you not only leave space

for them, but also satisfactory plumbing arrangements, i.e. T-connections in hot and cold water pipes instead of the usual elbow.

6 The kitchen will need to be supplied with hot and cold and drinking water. The hot water can be taken from the main hot water tank or from an instant gas heater or an electric storage heater, which can be located either in or adjacent to the kitchen. The drinking water must be straight from the mains supply and, except where the house has a water softener, this can also serve all the other kitchen needs. If there is a softener, then a softened cold water supply from a separate tap will be needed so that the benefits of soft water can be had for washing, etc.

1. The optimum arrangement – a fan set into a cooker hood over the hob.

2. This is a T-connection which gives the option of adding another appliance to those already plumbed in.

3. A veritable maze of pipes brings hot and cold water supplies to sinks, dishwasher and washing machine. Fortunately, all are tidily stowed away behind appliances and within cupboards – but are accessible if and when they need attention.

Materials

Floors

A kitchen floor takes a massive beating. It is walked on constantly, has grease and scraps of food dropped on to it, as well as water and other liquids. Occasionally, by mischance, it is flooded. Yet it is required to look good, be easy to clean, feel comfortable and warm to stand on for long periods, not be noisy or slippery and last for ever. Quite a specification!

Not all the materials described here conform in every detail, but some are so spectacularly attractive on one count that it may be worth putting up with their other deficiencies.

1. Black and white vinyl makes a smart and very fresh-looking floor which has the added advantage of not showing the dirt nearly so quickly as one plain colour.

2. John McConnell designed the interior of his large Victorian house so that the dining room is in the front, the kitchen at the back. Since there is no separation between the two, he decided that the good-quality boarded floor which he wanted to retain in the dining room must continue right through. Sanded to give a clean, smooth finish and then covered in a hard polyurethane lacquer, it has a warm, softly coloured quality which is becoming increasingly popular in kitchens.

Boarded floor

This is about as basic a floor as you can get, and in some older houses the boards are of good quality and, when cleaned, sanded and treated with either matt or glossy polyurethane, look very handsome. They can first be treated with a proprietary coloured stain if it is colour you are after. But in either case, natural or coloured, the boards *must* be treated with several coats of the polyurethane if they are not to wear thin and let grease and other dirt through to the wood below.

Test an area of wood first to ensure you are going to like the finished effect, and be aware that, though sanding machines can be hired for a reasonable cost, the dusty mess involved in doing such a job is considerable.

A boarded floor treated as described can be washed clean (with a damp rather than a wet cloth) and it has good, non-slip characteristics. It is inclined to be noisy and mats are advisable.

Hardwood floor

In a kitchen which opens directly off, or is even part of, a living room, it is sometimes possible to extend a general hardwood surface over the whole lot. This, whilst having

1

many of the characteristics of the softwood, boarded floor – being comfortable to walk on and good looking, but rather noisy – would be much tougher and have a longer life expectancy. With a surface treatment of polyurethane, it would also be relatively easy to keep clean.

With the advent of self-lay hardwood floors in strip, herringbone and mosaic patterns, it is a much less expensive proposition than it has been in the past. It does, however, have disadvantages besides those stated above. It is *not* impervious to flooding or to damage from very heavy wear and tear. Suitable woods (all available in ready-to-lay panels) would be maple which is exceptionally hardwearing, oak and pine amongst the pale woods, and teak, sapele and afzelia amongst darker woods.

Linoleum
Once upon a time, linoleum was used in kitchens up and down the land, but it has since been superseded by a variety of other, harder-wearing materials.

Cheap linoleum is still available in tawdry designs, but although it does not show the dirt in this form and is easily washed clean, its wearing properties are bad. It can only be considered as a makeshift and temporary surface.

Heavy-duty linoleum is another matter. Best laid by an expert, it is generally available only via contractors and not at the DIY shop (though manufacturers have recently been trying to rectify this constriction). It must be set on a smooth, nail-free surface and then will provide a soft, quiet, hardwearing floor. It is principally available in plain or flecked colours, the former showing dirt and scuff marks more than the latter, and can be simply washed clean. Housework addicts should resist polishing it if they want to avoid nasty accidents. This is an underused and underrated material that could easily make a comeback in kitchens if manufacturers were to come up with some dramatic colours.

Vinyl
It is vinyl which has superseded linoleum to a large extent, in both sheet and tile form.

Sheet vinyl is easy to lay, though again the under-

1

surface must be clean, dry and smooth. It is fairly quiet and soft, non-slip, does not show the dirt (mainly because it is heavily patterned) and is simply washed clean. It would survive a fair amount of water spillage and needs no polishing. This is a cheap product. More expensive and softer to walk on is sheet cushioned vinyl, which again is easy to lay, does not show the dirt, etc. It is also available now up to 4 m (13 ft) wide, which would involve little cutting and matching in the majority of kitchens.

My main complaint about these products, as about so many others, is on the design side, for they are almost universally designed to look like what they are not – parquet, marble, brick, terrazzo or ceramic tiles. A certain amount of this repro design (particularly when well done) is acceptable, but it would be good if even one manufacturer had the courage to produce vinyl sheeting with a good modern design which did not try to emulate something else.

Vinyl tiles suffer from a similar fault. But they are easy to handle and lay, and avoid wastage when only a small area is to be covered. They share all the properties of

1. Cork tiles with a vinyl skin surface really make the perfect kitchen floor, and industrial designer Jacek Basista chose them for the kitchen/dining room of the small Victorian house which he and his wife have converted. It's ideal for a busy working couple, but equally good for families with lots of children, since scuff marks, mud and bits of fluff barely show – and in any case can be quickly wiped away without hard scrubbing. Note also the splendid stainless steel work surfaces.

2. Designer Jon Wealleans's kitchen has a grey linoleum floor which is excellent for him since he is a bachelor, but might not be so good for family use as its pale colour tends to show the dirt. Note the simple let-down breakfast table, the specially made shutters to hide a bad view, and the various details which refer to his favourite period, the early years of this century.

2
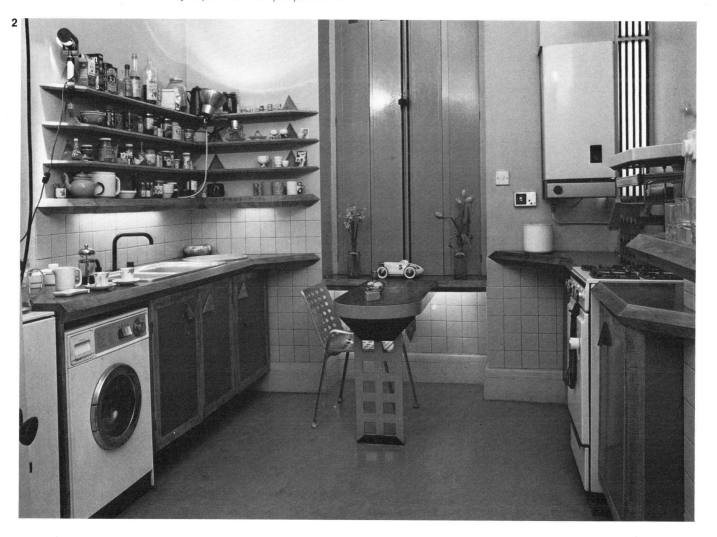

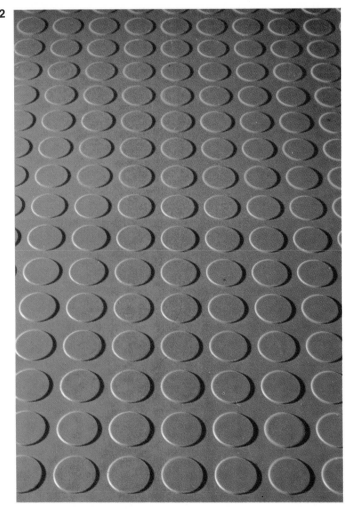

sheet vinyl, and in addition can be individually replaced in the event of damage. Also, it is possible to make patterns, including chequered effects, plain-coloured borders and so on.

Synthetic rubber

This flooring was originally intended for industrial use because of its excellent wearing properties. But these are no less appropriate in the home and since it is also quiet and soft to walk on, waterproof, non-slip and reasonably easy to wash clean, several manufacturers are now making a lighter-duty version, sized 600 × 600 mm (2 × 2 ft), in excellent plain colours which look superb in the kitchen setting.

High tech kitchens are nearly always floored in rubber. It should be laid by an expert and must go on smooth, clean, dry underfloors. Concrete screed is fine but a wooden sub-floor would probably need to be overlaid with ply or hardboard.

Cork tiles

Cork tiles look and feel warm, they are quiet to walk on, come in several pleasant shades of brown and can be laid on any floor surface provided it is dry, clean and smooth. They do not show the dirt, are easily washed clean and are reasonably non-slip. But they are not waterproof and are best sealed with polyurethane lacquer which will remedy this deficiency up to a point (though not in the event of flooding from a defective dishwasher, for instance).

A better option are cork tiles with a vinyl skin surface. Only a fraction of the cork's natural beauty is lost, but the tile is instantly much tougher in wear, never seems to look dirty and is swiftly cleaned by wiping with a damp cloth. More expensive than, for instance, vinyl, this kitchen flooring is one of the best looking and most practical available.

Ceramic tiles

These, in their various forms, look very beautiful in the kitchen. They are hardwearing, but they are also hard on the feet and noisy, and they are most suitably laid on a solid concrete sub-floor. Consult a manufacturer before laying them on a suspended wooden floor. Sometimes it is possible, but in this case a relatively inert material like blockboard must be put down first and a specially strong adhesive used.

Ceramic tiles come in two main types:

Quarries which are beloved by followers of the farmhouse kitchen style. They are available in various natural colours from pale cream to deep brown and look their best when polished, though some people prefer just to seal and wash them. A word of warning. From personal experience, I can tell you it is virtually impossible to seal the pale cream ones against the ravages of oil and grease. The stains made seep through the seal and are permanent thereafter. They can be treated with linseed oil but obviously this darkens them considerably and the whole point of the lovely cream colour is lost.

Glazed ceramic tiles are perfect in several respects: lovely colours, some beautiful designs (particularly the Italian ones), absolutely impervious to stains from grease or any other thing likely to be used in the kitchen, waterproof and easy to wash over. But they are expensive, noisy and some people find them hard on the feet. Consider your priorities.

Brick

This is another splendid material for kitchen flooring which is not so noisy as ceramics, and can be laid in several handsome patterns such as herringbone and basket weave (by an expert) as well as good natural colours. The bricks must be laid on a concrete sub-floor, though. They are rather hard to walk on and expensive, but can be sealed and washed or polished.

Marble

This is expensive, hard and cold and must be laid on a concrete sub-floor. But, conversely, it lasts a lifetime and looks beautiful. It does show the dirt though (fluff and breadcrumbs, if it is dark, mud and shoe scuffs if it is pale) and stains easily. But everyday dirt is easily washed away.

Slate

This is similar in most characteristics to marble, and is best for kitchen use with a non-slip riven surface.

Wall coverings

The simplest and cheapest wall covering is *paint* but this must be applied to a good, smooth, well-prepared surface. Poor plasterwork or other idiosyncrasies are best concealed by something more substantial. Gloss paint which is easily washable is most appropriate in the kitchen, although if you dislike a high-gloss finish vinyl emulsions are easier to clean than the old water-based ones.

If you are having a new kitchen built or renovating an old one and like the country look, you may choose to have one wall in exposed fair-faced *brickwork*. If you are exposing plastered bricks in an old house, test an area first to make sure they are worth exposing. Bricks may be

3

1. The rich, warm colours of quarry tiles have a universal appeal, and used here with wooden cupboards and cream paintwork, they erase any trace of coldness from what is nevertheless a thoroughly modern and functional kitchen.

2. Architects started using synthetic rubber tiles in their own homes when they found how good-tempered this material was in industrial and commercial settings. Apart from vivid green, they are available in many other good colours such as blue, dark green, cream, grey and black.

3. Carpet is bad in a kitchen because it can be quickly ruined, but when living room and kitchen are all one, it can work to create a clear division, as here, with glazed ceramic tiles on the kitchen floor contrasting sharply with soft carpeting at the living end of the room.

1

treated with several coats of clear emulsion so that they are easy to wash clean whilst still retaining their natural colour, or they may be covered in gloss or emulsion paint, when the colour is lost but the attractive texture retained.

A well-designed *wallpaper* makes a satisfactory and inexpensive wall covering in a room with a good extractor system, although it is not really suitable for the areas close to sinks and cooker. Ordinary wallpaper cannot be washed, however, and if the extractor fan is not good (or not present) the dirty deposits from cooking fumes would be unacceptable. *Vinyl-coated wallpapers* are more expensive but rather more appropriate in this overworked area because they can easily be wiped clean. Unfortunately, there are too many crude and unpleasant designs in this particular material.

There was a period when *tongued and grooved boarding* was the favourite treatment for at least one wall of a newly furbished kitchen. That particular fashion has been swept aside in the general enthusiasm for wooden-doored units. A case of too much of a good thing, perhaps . . . Nevertheless this type of wall covering is very practical where less than perfect walls are in question because it can conceal a multitude of

deficiencies. It looks warm and homely, it can easily be applied by a competent home decorator, and when sealed with a matt lacquer is impervious to dirt, though it will not take too many hard knocks and scratches without showing the signs. If you are lumbered with plastic-faced units, but want to bring some woody warmth to your kitchen, tongued and grooved boarding would be an easy solution.

Ceramic tiles, too, were once the epitome of luxury for kitchen walls: bright and colourful, easy to keep clean, relatively hardwearing – it was not difficult to see their appeal. They too have suffered from the general tendency to make less clinical-looking kitchens. They too, though, have singular merits, and they are really unbeatable as a wall surface for those places which are likely to be splashed with water and food; around the sinks, cooker and preparation area. It is difficult to find good strong plain colours and even more difficult to find modern designs, but they do exist (especially foreign products) and used in moderation make an efficient and good-looking wall covering.

Some of the wall coverings I have mentioned will meet certain needs, some will meet others. But do not make the mistake of using more than two or three in the same

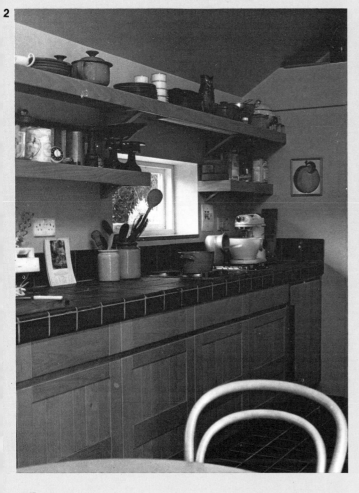

1. The owner of this kitchen designed her own tiles based on a charming eighteenth-century French design, and they were specially made for her by Rye Tiles. 2. Dark quarry tiles make a practical and handsome surface for both floor and worktops in Barry Gray's kitchen. The beech cupboards and table were made by ME Furniture. 3. Peter Bell is an architect who likes to use natural materials in the home. This kitchen has wooden storage units and exposed brick walls, though he wisely faced the area above the sinks with ceramic tiles. 4. This is a work surface in Andrew Holmes' kitchen. It is lined with white tiles, which are also used in the old kitchen-range recess where another work surface supports the portable electric oven he bought in the USA.

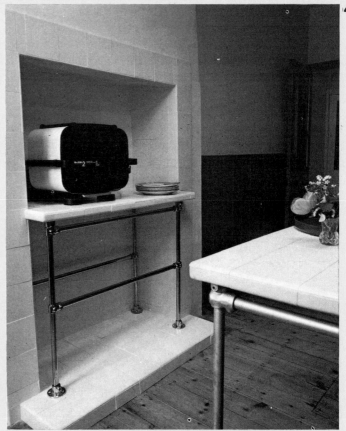

room or you will end up with a visual hotchpotch. Combine brick and wood, for instance, or gloss paint and wallpaper, or vinyl, tiles and emulsion paint, but not the whole lot together.

Work surfaces

The cleanest-looking and most hygienic kitchen work surface is *laminated plastic*, though I appreciate that there are reasons for choosing other materials. It is also, arguably, the best looking, and with reasonable care stays new and undamaged-looking for many years. Colours are reasonably good, and with the post-formed edges which are curved rather than right-angled, any hard, clinical connotations this material may have had no longer apply.

Unfortunately, the manufacturers have not been content to let it rest at that, but have gone overboard in the effort to produce strange and unconvincing reproductions of other materials. Wood, of course, was the first thing they copied in the effort to keep up with current fashion, and some of this, along with simulated linen or hessian, is fairly convincing. But when it comes to imitating onyx, raffia, tiles, slate and leather, some of it

1

textured to feel like the real thing, I begin to lose sympathy. It seems to reveal a foolish lack of confidence in the qualities of this excellent material. And so many of the materials emulated — leather, linen and raffia, for instance — would be completely inappropriate for kitchen work surfaces anyway.

But a plain, good quality plastic laminated surface with square or curved edges, or with wooden edges (some unit manufacturers offer this detail) is splendid.

Many people prefer real wood, and of course it must be *hardwood*. This is good as a chopping surface (one manufacturer actually makes a curved-edge inset to go with his plastic worktops for this purpose) but seems to lose its fresh, clean appearance too quickly for my taste. The stains, chips and scratches which appear are permanent once acquired, so that the kitchen never looks really clean again. However, many people are prepared to forego pristine looks for the undoubted natural charms of hardwood.

Marble, again, seems more suitable as a slab, inset for pastrymaking, into another type of surface. It undoubtedly looks handsome as a whole surface when new, but it is very expensive, and stains easily. A kitchen is no place for having to bother about leaving wet ring marks.

Stainless steel, though it loses its initial glitter over months of use as tiny scratches mar the surface, nevertheless acquires a softer sheen which is perfectly acceptable, and as its name implies it is certainly stainproof. It makes an excellent surface for standing hot pans, does not damage easily and will last for a very long time. There are no standard surfaces available in

2

this material (or in marble, come to that) which means they would have to be custom made, and therefore expensive. But a high tech enthusiast who does not object to diligent daily buffing with a soft cloth to remove smears, would make stainless steel first choice.

Ceramic tiles make a good if expensive work surface, and are suitably rustic looking for the farmhouse type of kitchen. They are impervious to both heat and dirt and unless something really heavy is crashed upon them from a great height, are unlikely to suffer damage. Good strong sealants are essential so that water cannot penetrate between tiles, but given that they will look good for many years. Be careful about colour and pattern, though. The gentle colours of quarry tiles are fine, but anything too strong and strident could quickly become offensive.

1. Architect Alan Tye chose stainless steel for all the work surfaces in his own kitchen, which opens directly into the dining room. Polished to a high glitter, it makes a striking serving table on the dining side, as well as providing a stain- and heat-proof surface in the kitchen.

2. A hefty wooden chopping-block is the best surface on which to chop vegetables, cut meat or slice fruit, for even a laminated plastic surface is liable to suffer damage from these activities. Hardwood just looks weathered and even more attractive with use and age.

3. Red plastics laminate work surface with post formed front edges compliments the crisp red cupboard edging to these Italian units.

3

Decoration

The choosing of equipment, planning and technical arrangements are all undoubtedly important aspects of kitchen design. What follows is, however, to many of us the most interesting element: decoration. It is also the most difficult to get right.

' You will realize that although I have tried to avoid laying down hard and fast rules about equipment, planning and so on, there are certain basic precepts to be followed which, allied with a dash of normal common sense, will guard you against glaring errors in these areas. The same does not apply when it comes to style and decoration, for here instinct and taste, both indefinable and elusive qualities, come into the picture. Lack of them can sorely affect results.

Most of the people who designed the kitchens illustrated in this book – by no means all of them professional designers – have both style and taste in large measure and for that reason their ideas are well worth studying, emulating and even, if they will forgive me for suggesting it, copying. Not copying *in toto*,

though, for every room must have an element of its owners if it is to be a complete success – indications of their likes, evidence of their lifestyle, and examples of the sort of decorative objects they have chosen and bought.

The decoration of a kitchen needs as much thought as does choosing the equipment. By that I mean overall thought, for it is pointless to choose various items such as wallpaper, floor covering and paint colour (however well they match and complement each other) if they do not work towards reaching some overall effect. For kitchen decoration, even more than the decoration of most other rooms, falls into several different styles, and every element in the room should be contributing to the style if a harmonious effect is going to be achieved.

Once you are aware of that fact, incipient sterility (for that is the danger) can be avoided by the addition of all the idiosyncratic odds and ends which most of us own and love. But the basic scheme and style should still shine through strong and clear.

I have deliberately not mentioned fashion. In kitchen

design, as in most other things now, fashion is a free-for-all. Though each decade has had a particularly strong influence at work – rows of built-in cupboards in the sixties, scrubbed pine and quarry tiles in the seventies, and a fragile movement towards high tech in the eighties – each and every one of these movements can be adapted and, handled well, look just as stylish and up-to-date as the next.

The kind of kitchen you choose will probably reflect the way you have decorated and chosen the rest of your house and will give a clue as to the sort of person (or family) you are. In case you are suffering from an identity crisis, here are general descriptions of some of the most potent types of decoration you could aim for.

Slick and modern

This is the sort of kitchen many of the manufacturers of kitchen equipment think they are illustrating in their advertisements. This was certainly so a few years back, when such illustrations had a wall-to-wall sweep of cupboards, topped by a gleaming plastic work surface, where hard tiles lined the walls and probably the floors, and where there was not an open shelf, unnecessary object or unchromed piece of equipment in sight.

That is not what I mean by slick and modern, and I certainly use the phrase in no pejorative sense. It describes a kitchen where the units are beautifully made (sometimes, though not essentially, specially designed and custom-built), with exceptionally good-quality surfaces, solid wood, granite or top-quality laminate for instance, and where the details are so refined and

The most successful kitchens follow a definite decorative style, such as high tech, of which architect Brian Taggart's, 1., is an excellent example. This view is looking towards the adjoining dining room which has been decorated in the same dramatic way: bright-red plastic surfaces, modern track lighting on a chromed wire fitting and, as a slightly atavistic contrast, rich cream paintwork. 2. Shows the dining end of Angela Chidgey's 'non-kitchen' style room. Practically everything in the room is arranged to draw your attention away from the fact that it is actually a working and very practical kitchen. There is pretty pottery arranged on open shelves, collections of baskets ranged around the walls, straw hats hanging from the ceiling, and bunch upon bunch of delicately coloured dried flowers. Comfortable sofas stacked with cushions are invitingly arranged near the big windows leading to the garden, and there is a huge wooden table which doubles as a surface for food preparation as well as for serving large-scale meals. Nevertheless, sinks, dishwashers, cookers and all the other paraphernalia of the kitchen are certainly present at the other end of this room (see page 21) although well tucked away amongst the non-kitcheny furniture. 3. A somewhat watered-down version of the farmhouse style kitchen, this large basement has been converted into a modern kitchen quite inexpensively by retaining the existing cupboards and dresser (not seen), and adding some inexpensive ready-made units and shelves. Pale quarry tiles bring lightness to what is by nature a somewhat dark room, exposed brickwork is painted the same cream as the rest of the room (white would have looked too bleak and bright in this setting), and though there are very crisp- and modern-looking table and chairs, the work surfaces are covered in quarry tiles.

perfect as to be virtually invisible. There are no crude handles, but either very discreet ones or a reliable push-to-open mechanism, concealed hinges, immaculate junctions between units and work surfaces, and sinks slipped into position with no visible surface joints at all. Wall tiles, if any (and this is by no means *de rigueur*), will probably be in a good plain colour, maybe white, and will be lined up exactly to match with any construction joints in cabinets. They will be expertly cut in around taps and other protuberances, and these taps (probably wall-mounted for ease of cleaning) will almost certainly be from one of the only two or three good modern ranges on the market. Stainless steel, marble and tiled work surfaces may also figure in this sort of kitchen.

Cookers and hobs will be of the most elegant and unobtrusive modern design, and the hob will probably be of the ceramic glass variety which gives a very smooth line. Naturally, every piece of equipment – the cooker, dishwasher, refrigerator, washing machine, etc. – will slot effortlessly and unobtrusively into the place which has been specially designed to receive it. Nowhere will there be awkward projections, unfilled slots of space, unfortunate junctions or dirt-collecting cracks, for this is the genuine modern McCoy.

Quality everywhere will be of the highest and the floor tiles will probably be of a hard material – quarry, hardwood or glazed white ceramic – to guard against

Precise detailing is of the essence in the 'slick and modern' kitchen, and the two kitchens shown on this page certainly have that, in their very different ways. The kitchen designed by architect John Guest, 1., has custom-made white units with aluminium trims, a white-tiled floor and chromed spotlights set on ceiling track. Equipment, such as ovens and refrigerators, is built into the walls, and the work surface is made of travertine marble. 2. has units made of beech (which also lines the walls), polished granite work surfaces and a pale hardwood floor. Discreet, simple and, alas, expensive, this kitchen is perfect to the last detail, including the beige ceiling inset with spotlights, matching beige blinds and sophisticated ceramic hob. Doors (not seen) are also painted glossy black.

2

accidental damage which would spoil the superlative overall effect.

Colours will probably be limited to a controlled one or two, but this does not mean they will not be strong and bold. Navy, bright red and grass green have all been used to great effect in this type of kitchen, as well as the ubiquitous white and dramatic black.

There will be wipe-clean blinds at the windows in a complementary colour, either plain or in an austere modern design. There will certainly be no jazzy pattern-ed curtains or dust-trapping venetian blinds.

Yes, there will be decorative objects, but extremely well-designed and carefully chosen ones, for the person who admires this style is hardly likely to go for pretty baubles or kitsch junk. These objects will be displayed and arranged so that they look their best, and they certainly will not be shoved around from place to place according to whim, nor will they be confined to cupboards. They will take their place on open shelves because they are meant to be seen.

Likewise, house plants will contribute to the careful picture of smooth elegance. They will not be a few dried-up wisps of fern or a tatty-looking spider plant; more likely there will be a dramatic (and expensive) palm placed to partially screen the eating area. And anything hanging in a basket will be in extravagant-looking profusion and certainly not hung with macramé streamers.

This style is superb when well done, but generally this is only by architects and designers, very high-grade ones at that. The do-it-yourself model is almost unheard of but my admiration for the amateur who succeeded in making it would be unbounded.

There is absolutely no reason why everyone should like this style, and I suspect that many people will not, but that a good many will be drawn to the next one.

The cottage kitchen

This does not have to be in a cottage. Quite probably it will be in a large suburban villa or a town flat, but its provenance will be unmistakable.

The kitchen units will of course be made in wood, preferably in dark oak veneer, and the cupboard doors will not be smooth faced, but decorated with mouldings and panels (not too decorated, I hope. See comments on this subject on page 18). There will almost certainly be a dresser, or at least cupboards with open shelves above to simulate a dresser, and the shelves will be laden with pretty, flower-patterned china.

The cooker will be free-standing, possibly an Aga in an attractive colour if the owner can run to this, and the colour will pick up one of the several pretty colours with which the whole room is decorated. Blue or turquoise, yellow, white and green in combination, pink, green and beige, or various shades of red. All look well against the dark oak, and china, floral curtains, the kitchen tablecloth (no nasty plastic surfaces here) and the tea towels, oven gloves and aprons will all be variously patterned in this way. There may also be thick lacy curtains of pristine whiteness at the windows and the table will possibly be surrounded by rush-seated chairs.

The work surfaces probably *will* be in plastic for, cottagey or not, this is a new and functional kitchen, but the edges will be softly curved and the plastic will be patterned to simulate something else, linen being the

1. **John and Joy Dievel have lined the ceiling of their cottage kitchen with wood, and bought inexpensive wooden kitchen units to give themselves plenty of storage. Pieces of marble which they picked up in second-hand shops act as work surfaces, and the shelves are filled with Joy's collections of old china, copper and old-fashioned kitchen utensils. They retained the existing quarry-tiled floor and used some of their collection of pretty old bentwood chairs around the marble-topped table.**

2. **Another cottage kitchen is furnished with a high-quality range of ready-made dark pine kitchen units, some of them with glass-fronted doors; this is an old-fashioned way of displaying pretty china without it constantly becoming coated with dirt, and it is becoming increasingly popular again in the modern kitchen. An old-fashioned oil lamp hangs over the table, the space beneath is used to store wine, and there are beautiful hexagonal quarry tiles on the floor.**

most attractive simulation. I refuse to even consider the possibility of simulated onyx, reeds or cork, though they are certainly available.

There will be flower-printed wallpaper on the walls, geraniums in terracotta pots on the window sills, lots of pottery on the shelves, and the very minumum of tiles around the sink and other wet areas. A few copper pans will probably be hung on the walls, and they will be for decoration rather than use.

The floor, if the owner can afford it and the structure is strong enough to bear the weight, will be in a herringbone-patterned brick (treated to make cleaning easy), or if money is short it could be simply floorboards, stripped, sanded and varnished, in which case there will

be rush mats at salient points. Vinyl tiles are another possibility, and they will almost certainly, though of good intrinsic quality, emulate bricks, quarry tiles or something equally traditional.

The equipment will be well designed and modern, but not glaringly so, and whenever possible the ovens, refrigerator, dishwasher and so on will have coloured doors to make them less obtrusive and more homely. Or they will be concealed behind panels of a similar material to the unit doors. The sinks and drainers too will probably be in coloured enamel and only the taps are likely to strike an untoward and ill-conceived chrome note. A clever and prosperous owner may, however, light upon the excellent copies of Edwardian brass-head taps

which are available, or on the excellent modern design which is available in brass.

At its best this style of kitchen can be charming. It is rarely designed by architects or designers for themselves, and not voluntarily for their customers, but often and most successfully by women for their own homes. There is no reason why it should not be every bit as functional as the previous type of kitchen, even though it looks so totally different.

High tech

The high tech kitchen is about as far removed from the cottagey one as can be imagined. Even though the high tech style has been around for several years now, certainly since 1978 when the book *High Tech* was first published in the USA, it has never become a really important force except amongst a few *cognoscenti* who live mainly in the world's capitals, and are mostly architects and designers. The high tech style is based on components which were designed for other, mainly industrial, purposes; for the factory, the warehouse, the hospital, the building site or even the street.

Do not assume that this is necessarily an inexpensive way to construct a kitchen. These products, many of them in stainless steel, glass, chromed metal and aluminium, have an austere and functional quality which is often extremely beautiful, but they are manufactured to a high standard of design and finish which

tends to be expensive. Against this, they are by their nature hardwearing, easily cleaned, aesthetically pleasing and – though some are of old and classic design – look innovative and original.

A high tech kitchen will have very plain cupboards, painted in a dark colour, and though these may be a system designed and intended for use in a laboratory or store room, they could equally well be standard kitchen units of a good, simple design. There will also be a good deal of open shelving. This will either be the chromed wire variety commonly used in industrial kitchens, the slotted angle system (Dexion) that you will see in garages and which also has plastic bins clipped to wall-hung louvred backplates, or simple metal library shelves.

1. This cottage kitchen is full of warmth and colour and country things: plants and jugs of cottage flowers, a brick floor covered with a pretty rug, exposed brick walls and old-fashioned stick-backed chairs. But modern facilities are there too. Note the ample power outlets, the inset hob and the stainless steel sink.

2. Architect Brian Taggart's high tech kitchen/dining room. High-level shelves are made of a proprietary chromed wire system (other components of which form the frame for the central island unit), and there are red plastic work surfaces above the cupboards, which were specially made with doors of an aluminium construction. The design is sharpened by black plastic trim and door handles. Red plastic-coated metal dining chairs stack at one end of the island unit when not in use. Tubes carrying spotlights are fixed to a length of chromed wire shelving suspended from the ceiling through kitchen and dining ends of the room.

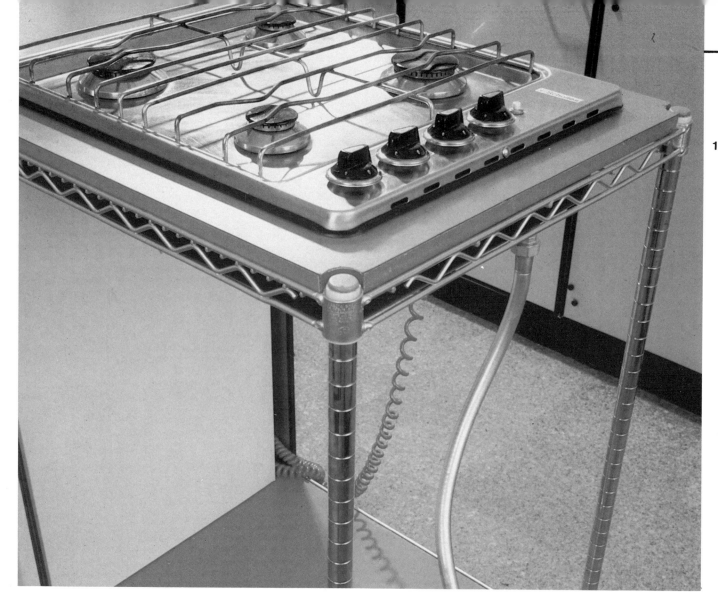

Work surfaces may be in a plain laminated plastic – what could be more industrial than that? But more likely, in keeping with the rest of the room, they will be in stainless steel, heavy-duty linoleum or – somewhat impractically – in studded synthetic rubber whose surface is not quite even enough for the purpose. Any of these materials will be used to line walls around the wet areas, and elsewhere the walls will be covered in a beautifully finished surface of high-gloss paint.

Studded rubber will most probably be used on the floor, and here it is an excellent, handsome and hardwearing material. Other possible floor coverings are heavy-duty linoleum or glazed ceramic tiles with a cheap alternative being duckboards on a simple boarded floor.

Appliances will be of the most basic, least 'got-up' type, and passionate devotees of the style whose cash is equal to their enthusiasm may go to the lengths of purchasing large-scale catering cookers, dishwashers and refrigerators which, made in stainless steel with heavy glass doors, have a gutsy bravura totally in accord with the style.

Windows will be clad in plain roller blinds or wooden shutters, and dining tables will, if not made of enamelled metal such as were once used in factory canteens, have

steel frames inset with tough wired glass tops. Metal chairs, or stools, of which there are several well-designed modern examples on the market, will be the natural complement to tables of this nature.

Industrial lampshades made of steel have long been popular with designers for their direct, unequivocal shapes and they are the obvious choice for the high tech kitchen. Energy-saving fluorescent tubing, frankly displayed and sometimes worked into unexpected shapes, will also have a place, as will massive-looking bulkhead lights such as are used on service stairways and in warehouses.

Equally unconcealed will be many of the service pipes we have been learning to 'lose' over the past fifty years. They will not, however, flaunt themselves exactly as the builder's merchant left them, but electric power-cables will be channelled through brightly painted exposed conduits, heating ducts and extractor ducts will form sculptural shapes across the ceiling and radiators and hot-water pipes will contribute their shapes to the general aesthetic in a blatant and even dominant fashion.

Colours? On the whole, these tend towards the industrial greys, black and white from which the whole style emanated, but when colour is present it is bold and primary and fresh. Bright yellow crockery and saucepans sing out, set against a monotone background. Or vivid red ducting adds to the drama of an otherwise black-and-white room. Or bright green rubber flooring and green paintwork make a foil for chromed wire shelving and stainless steel surfaces.

A high tech kitchen will have few decorative objects, and such as there are will be limited to those with an industrial origin: factory-type wall clocks, glass laboratory jars and flasks, glass bricks and stainless steel jugs. Cooking utensils, often purchased from industrial catering shops, will hang from chromed wire wall-racks or be stored in wire pull-out drawers.

The high tech kitchen is no cosy womb to which members of a family gravitate for comfort. Rather it is a machine shop, designed to stimulate, spur and refresh.

Farmhouse style

Over a number of years, this has probably become the most popular style of them all. Kitchens in inner-city apartments, in new town estates and in Edwardian terraced houses have all been got up to emulate what their owners think of as the interiors favoured by farming families. Again, designers started the trend, but in the face of its overwhelming popularity and, often, ruination, they have moved on to trendier pastures.

The farmhouse kitchen should I think only be attempted where there is ample space, for its components are large, square and chunky, and look ridiculous stuffed into a slot of a room in a tower block. But big square basement rooms in town houses work well; so do sculleries and kitchens in terraced houses which have been opened up to form one fairly large dining-kitchen. Even a modern estate house kitchen can, if it is large enough, be given a semblance of character and bucolic charm with this style.

1. This is a close-up view of the island unit in Brian Taggart's high tech kitchen. It shows the frame, constructed from components of the chromed shelving system he has used on the walls. The inset gas hob with exposed piping demonstrates the aesthetic potential of the high tech ethos when handled skilfully. The plastic-coated cork tiles on the floor are not really in character, but were Taggart's concession to family life.

2. This spacious farmhouse style kitchen is in a new extension to an old house where there was ample room for all the pine cupboards and massive pine dining table which its owners required, plus a big pine dresser for displaying china. The original stonework of the old house, left exposed and painted, can be seen at the rear, and there is the customary quarry-tiled floor. Wooden ceiling beams were left exposed, and though the modern spotlights which light the room are not quite what one would expect in this style of kitchen, they do an excellent lighting job.

2

The whole essence of the thing is to choose natural materials – wood, brick and ceramic are the main constituents. The kitchen units will all be in wood of course, preferably pine, and the working surfaces will be of solid hardwood with a slab of marble inset for pastrymaking. There will be another inset, probably of a different hardwood, made for chopping. For much *real* cooking goes on here, unlike the quick heating-up, defrosting and de-canning which is endemic to some of the other styles.

A big stripped pine table will sit in the centre of the room (you see why there must be plenty of space?) and this will be surrounded by old chairs picked up in junk shops, or it may be set to one side of the room with stripped pine church pews set against the wall for seating. A butcher's chopping block, either a genuine one cast out by some butcher, or one of the modern reproductions, is also likely to feature in the farmhouse kitchen.

The floors will preferably be quarry tiled, though cork could take the place of tiles where the floor structure or finance is not up to them, and quarry tiles will form splashbacks around the sink and cooker. Other wall surfaces will either be of exposed brick in its natural state or painted cream, or they will be plastered and painted in cream gloss paint. All the surfaces which appear so old fashioned – bricks, wood and tiles – will, unlike the genuine old-fashioned article, be perfectly easy to keep clean because they will be treated with layers of matt polyurethane lacquer.

Modern equipment fits a little awkwardly into this pastoral idyll and some proponents will go as far as installing deep-glazed ceramic sinks (searching out elderly brass cross-head taps to go with them) and Aga cookers. The refrigerator and washing appliances will be hidden away in cupboards or laundry rooms. But in any case the equipment will be chosen in as earthy colours as are available, and gas, which has an indefinably rural quality, will be preferable to electricity.

A converted oil lamp will provide lighting for the table – even an unconverted one in some extreme cases – and others will hang from the ceiling to provide overall light, but the sensible farmhouse kitchen owner will also have practical fluorescent tubes concealed above the work surfaces.

If a large, cold, walk-in larder can be contrived it certainly will, and this will have the prescriptive marble shelves, if not the sides of bacon hanging from above.

Colour will not play a strong part in the decoration of the farmhouse kitchen and will reside mainly in the gentle creams and browns of the natural materials.

Paintwork will never be white, but will be that soft, deep colour so reminiscent of farmhouse cream. Most accessories will be in wood or ceramic – there will be wooden draining racks (now widely available in the shops), ceramic jars filled with wooden spoons on the worktops, wooden shelves on the walls filled with pretty pots and jars, and a wooden roller-towel rail on the back of the kitchen door.

Cotton curtains will be in soft muted colours to fit in with the generally gentle colour scheme. They may be brown and white, or cream and green, or in different

shades of brown; and if they are not in a small floral print they are likely to be checked. Bunches of dried flowers and herbs will hang from the ceiling, and there may be herbs growing in pots on the window sills. Pressed and dried flowers, made into pictures and framed, will often hang around the walls.

Cheerful and welcoming though it is intended to be, the farmhouse style can, if taken to extremes, be cloying in its intensity and offputting in its somewhat hypocritical emphasis on harking back to the natural and, by implication, good life.

Though Angela Chidgey's kitchen is in London it has very definite 'farmhouse' leanings. There is a plethora of pine, a lovely warm cork floor, a discreet brown-enamelled sink and many country baskets scattered about, some of them full of fruit. Size is, of course, an essential element in the farmhouse style, and this is a very large room.

The open kitchen

This is the kitchen style which I personally like the least of all, though I can admire it in an objective fashion. It is the room where everything, but everything, is open to view.

All the owners' possessions will be ranged on open shelves – groceries at high level, saucepans and casseroles lower down, and pottery and china in huge open dresser-type fittings. Cooking knives are slotted into racks along the walls, wooden implements stand in pots on the work surfaces, and there is often a huge rack suspended over the cooking area which is laden with cooking implements.

Now the whole essence of this room is in the arrangement of each item. The spice packet, half open, will not be chucked back on to the shelf all anyhow. It will be in pristine condition and take its place in the exact position where it will contribute to a carefully contrived still-life. And everything else in the room will be there on the same basis; the pots making patterns, the jars glittering in rows, the vegetables heaped colourfully in open racks and the spaghetti packets chosen for their graphics rather than the quality of their contents.

The equipment and surfaces in this room will be of secondary importance since they are visually overwhelmed by everything else, and since in any case function is very much subordinate to appearances. This style will, in fact, often be used as a device to detract from the appearance of elderly equipment, shabby walls and worn floor covering.

Of extraneous decoration, such as pot plants, pictures and the like, there will be virtually none, since it would be superfluous, and the eating area will be of the simplest unadorned kind for the same reason. There will probably be a cheap, plastic-topped table of the sort found in downmarket coffee shops, and matching chairs. True to form, the pepper and salt pots, probably mustard and pickle jars too, and a small pot of flowers,

will make some sort of decorative statement on this table whether a meal is in progress or not.

Lighting will be most carefully planned, and will often take the form of track lighting set across the ceiling with the spots directed towards particularly successful arrangements – the many different-coloured sugars in their row of glass jars, the packets of tea mounded to make a satisfying pattern, the rich blue enamelled saucepans ranged along one wall. The walls themselves are often lined with sheets of pegboard or cork which not only serve to hide any deficiencies in their decoration, but facilitate display arrangements.

There is one big drawback – and this is why I am not keen. All these open shelves and their contents, however beautifully arranged, are likely to get coated very soon in a greasy film from the fumes generated in kitchens. So here more than in any other type of kitchen a powerful fan extractor is essential. Given that, and an immaculately tidy and visually alert family, the result can be great.

1. Here most of the cooking pots, utensils and crockery are stored on open shelves (see also the green-painted dresser shown in the photograph on page 19). A wire wall-rack hangs over the work surface into which are set sink, drainer, hob and marble pastry-making slab, and this is hung with a carefully worked-out arrangement of pans and implements. Note that this sort of storage arrangement can be disastrous if it is allowed to become untidy.

2. Barry Weaver has also chosen an open storage arrangement for his tiny kitchen, and managed to achieve a little more space by taking his wooden shelves right across the window. There are such beautiful kitchen goods available nowadays – in brightly coloured plastics, wood, pottery and enamel – that it is very tempting, providing you have an innate sense of order and self-discipline plus good visual sense, to emulate this method of storage, but a few dented pans covered in grime and shoved on to a shelf all anyhow will certainly not have the desired effect.

The non-kitchen

This style would suit a variety of situations and people. It would suit those who have to live and cook all in one room. That includes the occupants of a small house who want to knock all the ground-floor rooms into one, as well as bed-sitter dwellers. It would suit those who are hard up and not able to afford expensive units and equipment, and it would also suit the not-so-tidy ones who do not feel up to keeping their kitchens in a state of frozen perfection.

The non-kitchen will not look particularly like a kitchen. Its storage units will not be specially designed or bought from a well-known manufacturer, but will consist of old chiffonniers, obsolete filing-cabinets, dressers, sideboards or desks. The table for eating will probably be an old dining table, not one specially designed for kitchen use, and likewise the chairs will be a motley assortment from the local junk shop.

The sinks may be new or second hand, according to the financial status of their owner, but in either case they will be set into a piece of furniture which was designed for some other use – a sideboard or wash stand for instance. And the equipment, even if new, will not proclaim its glossy, enamelled presence too brazenly but will be tucked away within a cupboard, if it is a dishwasher; painted an unexpected colour, if it is a refrigerator; or unobtrusively positioned, if it is a cooker.

If all this sounds formidably scrappy and unattractive, wait for the rest. This kitchen should not be simply a collection of disparate junk. Each item will have been carefully hunted down to go with the next and, though every piece of furniture will not necessarily be of the same period, it often will be, and preferably made of similar material. Sometimes, in fact, period is an important factor, with Art Deco being a strong runner for favourite style. The whole lot will be arranged in logical sequence to determine work patterns, and then work surfaces will be constructed of some sympathetic linking material like hardwood or marble which will not have instant kitchen connotations.

In the case of the impoverished exponents of this type of kitchen, the furniture may verge on the junky and be in poor condition. In this case it will be painstakingly repaired and linked to its fellows by several coats of gloss paint in a good colour. Walls will not be tiled, but lined in a beautifully patterned wallpaper which if not vinyl coated by its makers (and few vinyl-coated papers are of really good design) will be covered in several coats of a matt varnish around the sink and cooking areas.

Top-quality lighting may be sacrificed to the general effect, but there will be attractive non-kitcheny looking pendant lights hanging centrally and over the eating area with, if the owner is sensible, at least a couple of wall-mounted spots directed towards the work areas.

The floor may be stripped, sanded and varnished boards, or it may be covered in vinyl patterned to look like a travertine marble or provençal tiles, or the bare boards may be stained in one of the rich colours available for this purpose, but in any case it will have several washable rugs (laid on non-slip netting) of the type suitable for use in any room in the house.

Wood-framed oil paintings will hang on the walls, there will be vases of flowers rather than pot-plants, and curtains may be in some material such as lawn which is not normally associated with kitchen use. The colour schemes too will be quite unexpected; pink and red, varying shades of yellow, or purple and lime green.

Though architects and designers will shy away from treating a room or area in this fashion, their logical minds revolting at the element of chance and opportunism in its creation, imaginative and patient people of other persuasions often bring it off surprisingly well.

Not one of these kitchen types may appeal to you. You may have a predilection for something totally different. But they are intended to give some ideas, start you thinking and help towards the purpose of achieving an overall coherence and design consistency.

1

2

3

On the previous page is a kitchen in a rather dark block of Edwardian mansion flats. To lift its spirits – and its owner's too – existing cupboards and open shelves were painted bright red, some more were added, and the walls lined with black tiles, grouted white. This particular treatment of the 'open kitchen' style worked well in this case, whereas rows of cupboards with doors would have only emphasized the gloom.

There is no one answer to the problem of designing a kitchen, and those which are indelibly stamped with the owner's personality are often the most successful. The three shown here are completely different in every way, but each works well for its owner. 1. Garden designer John Brookes lived in a basement flat for a short period, with a combined kitchen/living room. The kitchen is simply fitted with inexpensive units which are enlivened by china decorated with the flowers and fruit redolent of the country for which its owner was pining at that time. A plaster pillar, picked up in a junk shop, separates the two areas in a charmingly idiosyncratic way. 2. Painter Chloe Cheese's free-standing, brightly coloured kitchen is ideal for her large studio flat and relaxed lifestyle. 3. Designer Michael Baumgarten has a studio flat in the same converted warehouse, but his kitchen – linked to a central storage block in the great open room – is very different and consists of no more than wooden cupboards and work surface in which are incorporated hobs and sink, the oven and refrigerator being housed in the storage block on the left.

BATHROOMS

Equipment

Choosing what you will put into a bathroom is much more straightforward than equipping a kitchen. The main furniture has really changed very little since bathrooms first came into use. It comprises a bath, a wash bowl, a lavatory, a shower, and taps for the bath and shower. The only items to make recent entries on the scene are bidets and, more recently, built-in storage. Not so many people go overboard fitting out a bathroom with unnecessary pieces of equipment as do for kitchens, partly because there is just not so much with which to be seduced. The one thing which does tend to squat clean and unused in the corner of some bathrooms is the bidet, a continental delight which for some reason the British have not flocked to use – though many have bought one. However fastidious you may be, however many times a day you may *wish* to wash your bottom, if you spend most of your time away from home – at work, school and play – then the bidet will be of limited use, even as a foot bath (for which the Council of British Ceramic Sanitaryware Manufacturers are, rather desperately I fear, suggesting it). If you are often at home, then it is a good and hygienic addition to the daily bath routine.

So having decided for or against the bidet, you have also to choose the bath, a lavatory, a wash bowl and, if there is room, a shower. On pages 112–13 we go into the question of separate shower rooms, with various suggestions as to where they can be located, but if there is no room for this additional facility, at least try to fit a shower into the main bathroom. If the bathroom is used by more than one person, and most are, this will speed up the day's major ablutionary sessions as well as saving water. And unless the men you know are different from the men I know, they will prefer a shower to a bath.

Incidentally, certain establishments, for instance bachelor flats, could well manage without a bathroom and simply have a shower room, but for the purposes of this book I will assume a bathroom to include, by definition, a bath.

The only other major puchase for a bathroom, but one which is often neglected, is a means for storage, and as we shall see this can nowadays take the form of fitted units similar to those designed for kitchens.

Just one word about colour. Sanitaryware is available now in many deep and glowing shades, as well as those slightly nauseous pastels with which builders of speculative houses sought to woo their customers in the early postwar years – 'bathroom with *coloured* suite'. Admittedly these rich new colours are preferable, but there are a few points to bear in mind before you select one. Remember that you will now be tied to one colour scheme for the foreseeable future unless you can face

1. This is a traditional porcelain-enamelled cast-iron bath with a wide flat bottom and a drop front which some elderly or infirm people find easier to use. Measuring 1700 × 750 mm (67 × 29½ in), it is of ample proportions and has all the strength associated with cast-iron, as well as being available in several good strong colours including harvest gold.

2. The manufacturers claim that this corner bath can easily fit into a bathroom measuring only 1695 × 2745 mm (55 × 108 in), which would make it a candidate for many average family bathrooms. It does not, as many corner baths do, require an inordinate amount of hot water for comfortable bathing, and the integral seat would be attractive to the elderly, the children or anyone who just wants to cut his toe-nails in comfort. Made of acrylic, this bath comes in several colours, including bright-blue and avocado, and its bulging side panel is designed to facilitate cleaning – which I can see might be a problem.

the expense of changing all the sanitaryware. Secondly, you must make up your mind to a fair amount of extra cleaning, for soap splashes and hard-water deposits do proclaim their presence most aggressively against these strong backgrounds. And thirdly, be sure to get all items from the same manufacturer if possible, for there is likely to be more than a slight variation in colour between various makes.

Some firms are now making their wares with a shaded effect – the bath for instance starting off deep brown at the rim and shading to coffee at the base – but this gives a restless and gimmicky appearance which I cannot imagine will have much popular appeal.

Baths

What do you want your bath to be made of? Traditionally, it will be cast-iron or pressed steel with a vitreous enamel finish. These baths are quality products which will last a lifetime and are liable to be damaged only by chipping. The quality of the enamel is such that you would have to chisel away quite ferociously before you had much effect. These baths come in a reasonable range of colours, as well as white, but generally only in standard shapes including the wide, flat-bottomed type which is generally recommended as being suitable for elderly people and for use with an integral shower. They do not, generally speaking, include the more flamboyant shapes: corner baths, double baths, circular baths, baths with seats, and baths variously described as oriental soaking tubs, massage tubs or Japanese baths.

These, more usually, are made in acrylic or grp (glass reinforced polyester e.g. Fibreglass). The colour range is excellent (although the enamelled bath manufacturers have practically caught up in this respect) and grp baths do lend themselves to decoration in the form of fabric, paint or other decorative substance, bonded into the surface. Since these applications are almost universally beastly in design, I do not propose to discuss them any more, except to say that if your taste runs to such exotica this really is the wrong book for you. There is, however, one extremely beautiful grp bath. This is an exact reproduction in plain white of the free-standing baths with claw feet which were in use during the early part of this century.

Manufacturers have, on the whole, exploited the malleable properties of acrylic to much better advantage. With it they have been able to produce baths in all the shapes mentioned (and in others too), they have been able to impart the most dazzling colours and they have been able to do these things at considerably lower prices than those charged for steel and iron baths.

2

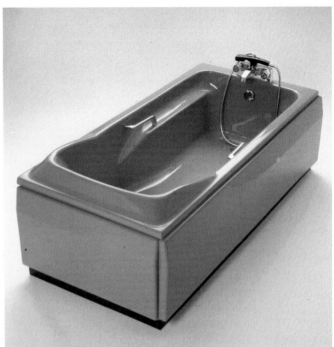

But there are pros and cons for each material.. The advantages of steel baths, apart from their durability, are that they feel comfortingly solid and rigid, and do not move, cracking adjacent tiles or dislodging waterproof seal as they do so.

Acrylic baths, as well as being cheaper, are light and easy to install (one designer whose bathroom is featured in this book fetched his own bath from the showroom, put it on the roof of his car, carried it upstairs when he reached home and installed it single-handed), they are warm to sit upon and easy to clean. But they are subject to cigarette burns (if bathtime smoking is your vice), they scratch easily and unless very carefully installed in the steel frame provided by the manufacturer, they are apt to wobble disconcertingly as you scramble in.

Other things to consider when buying a bath are:

1 A slip-proof surface on the base is a good idea, most particularly if you are infirm or elderly.
2 As long as a bath has grab rails to which they can cling, low-sided models are good for the infirm and elderly. An excellent alternative is a vertical pole, firmly fixed between floor and ceiling close to the bath.
3 Some elderly people would rather cope without rails, preferring to have a *high*-sided bath, and leaning on the high side to support themselves as they get in.
4 If you are neither elderly nor infirm but would like grab rails anyway, make sure by sitting in the bath of your choice that any rails are in the right place for *your* comfort.

5 Be sure that tap positions are exactly where you want them. Some baths have no holes, or can be specially ordered with no holes, and you drill your own where you want them. This seems the ideal way, for then you can decide whether to have taps at either end, at the side, or better still (for it makes cleaning easier) projecting from the wall above.
6 Many baths can be bought with matching grp side panels. They may suit your purposes well if you have no other ideas about boxing-in the bath. But there are alternatives which I shall mention in the chapter on decoration and since these ready-made panels are not the most beautiful objects – in fact some are grossly overblown and ugly – they are generally to be avoided.

Wash bowls

You will want one wash bowl in your bathroom. You may easily want two. Again, there are several different materials you can choose from: traditional vitreous china, acrylic, reconstituted stone and, surprisingly, you may think, there is stainless steel. Normally relegated to the kitchen, stainless steel had long been used for wash bowls in industrial buildings, and along with other things formerly associated with that world it is joining the high tech movement into the bathroom, in the shape of some particularly handsome wash bowls and lavatories. The stainless steel products do, as I have said in another chapter, need rather more cleaning than their name implies to keep them in spotless condition, and they

3

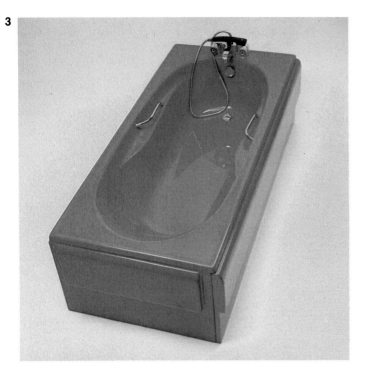

4

gradually acquire a patina of tiny scratches with use. Nevertheless, this is a hardwearing and hygienic material to be used if you are into the high tech ethos.

So you choose between china and acrylic (with roughly the same pros and cons as those applying to baths) or steel. Or you may opt for the less obvious reconstituted stone which seems to have no disadvantages except that it is expensive, or Corian, a marvellously versatile material made by Dupont. This looks like marble and can be worked like wood. It is stain-resistant, any scratches and burns can usually be removed with abrasive cleaners, and it is available in ready-made form as a vanitory top with bowl, or it can be purchased in slab form and worked to your particular requirements.

1. This splendid and capacious bath, complete with claw feet and gold-plated taps, is an exact reproduction in grp (Fibreglass reinforced plastic) of the free-standing baths in use years ago. But it is not a proposition for the small bathroom, and it is expensive.

Manufacturers of acrylic baths have certainly exploited this material's potential in terms of both shape and colour. Since acrylic baths are light and therefore easy to install, and less expensive than steel or cast-iron, they have become popular with those who have to watch costs and those who are doing much of the work themselves. The models on this page all come from the same manufacturers, and are available in a range of good, strong colours including the ones shown.

2. The Michelangelo measures 1700 × 800 mm (67 × 32 in) and has a high, raised back which would give added comfort to those who read in the bath. 3. The Brasilia bath measures 1800 × 800 mm (71 × 32 in), and has a sloping back and hand grips. 4. The Lido is a corner bath, one of the newest in this manufacturer's range. It has a shallow seat/shelf. 5. Nagoya measures a spacious 1850 × 1050 mm (73 × 41 in) and, with a back rest at both ends, is designed to allow two people to bath together. Because of its sloping shape, the manufacturers claim that less water is required than is usually the case in a double bath.

5

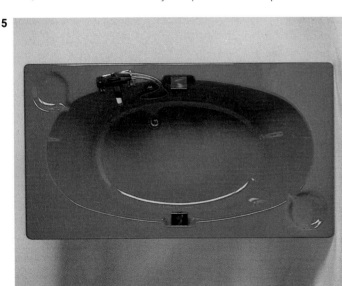

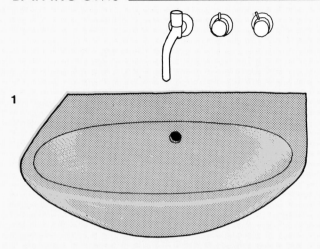

Your wash bowl can be wall fixed, with its attendant piping concealed by a pedestal, but even the best-designed of this type tends to look like a gawky afterthought. Wall-hung bowls are better, especially if they are positioned so that their pipework is not too apparent; sadly, the one design of this sort which had the pipes totally concealed within its own bulk in a wonderfully sculptural shape, is no longer available.

By far the best arrangement is to have the bowl built into a vanitory unit or work surface. Pipes vanish, splashes are easily wiped clean, and the surface holds all the bathroom paraphernalia. If there are cupboards beneath, so much the better.

There are bowls of various sizes and shapes to fit all these situations. Buy the biggest you have room for because this makes washing – yourself, your under-wear, your hair, your hairbrushes or even the baby – so much easier and less splashy. Choose one which has a simple, uncomplicated shape which will be easy to clean, and – particularly if you are not building it into a shelf or vanitory unit – choose one with as generous a rim as possible on which to perch the soap powders, shampoos, mascaras and so on which go with bath-room activities. There should also be soap recesses. It is amazing how many basins are made without this seemingly essential facility – essential, that is, unless you fancy a separate soap dish which too often ends up as a revolting pool of slimy water, or one of those slightly aggressive-looking magnetic soap holders.

Again, the question of tap-holes arises. As with baths, it is best to choose a bowl which enables you to place them where *you* want them, and not where the manufacturer dictates.

Taps

This brings me to the subject of taps, and here I must confess to being a purist. As indicated elsewhere, I do not like most of the taps currently on the market, and those specifically offered for bathrooms seem to be amongst the worse. A great blob of acrylic is not easily operated with a soapy hand, but that is what many of

them have. Hard angles, for psychological as well as physical reasons, are not appropriate in the bathroom. Heavily faceted chrome is quickly corroded, especially in hard-water areas. And try cleaning within the tight curves of some of those ornate mixers, or in the space beneath many of the strangely angled spouts.

I long for elegant and simple designs which will look good and be easy to wipe clean. The beautifully simple Danish taps which are available in a chrome or brass finish as well as several brilliant colours, the pale grey plastic taps and the reproductions of Edwardian cross-head taps were all mentioned in the kitchen section. All, in their very different ways, conform to this specification and all are equally suitable for the bathroom, along with just a few of the general run of chromium-plated taps which are on the market. Many of the most expensive taps also have a gold-plated version, but gold plating does nothing to conceal the intrinsic deficiencies in their design.

If the edge of the bath or bowl is sufficiently close to the wall, taps can be set into the wall itself which makes a very much easier cleaning detail, but with a wide rim to the bath or bowl this is not always possible. When taps are to be fixed to the rim of bath or bowl avoid setting them back too close against the wall or to each other, thus creating a muck trap, and similarly if there is a lever for a waste-trap (as opposed to a chain and plug) keep that well separate from the taps.

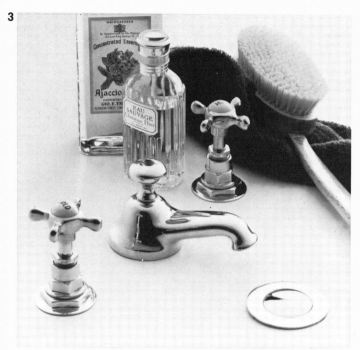

1. Two tap arrangements. On the left is probably the best of all, with the taps wall-mounted so that there is nothing to prevent easy cleaning of the wash bowl. On the right, simple cross-head controls, with a combined spout/pop-up waste control, are well separated so that the spaces between are easily cleaned.

2. This basin, designed to be set into a vanitory unit or shelf, is made of vitreous china and has a neat chrome trim which avoids any danger of water seepage, despite the fact that it is flush with the surface. It measures 540 × 440 mm (21⅝ × 17⅜ in) and is available in many colours, strong as well as pale.

3. These are amongst the most beautiful of the Edwardian reproduction taps on the market. Manufactured in solid brass and gun-metal, and finished in polished brass, chrome or gold plate, they are of excellent quality. Besides the basin set with pop-up waste shown here, the range includes stand-up taps, bath and hand-shower mixer and bath filler.

4. The Optima ceramic wash bowl can be set into a vanitory unit or shelf. It measures 620 × 460 mm (24⅖ × 18 in) and is available for use with separate taps or with single-hole or three-hole mixers.

Lavatories

These are normally only made in vitreous china, though there is a particularly good-looking stainless steel one in the industrial range mentioned on page 90. The vitreous china ones come in all colours to match the baths, bowls and so on from their manufacturers' ranges. (At least one such range is rather crudely decorated with flowers, and this includes the loo.) Functionally, there are two options: syphonic flushes, which are quiet and with a very positive flush, or wash-down flushes which take up less space and are cheaper.

Lavatories come in three basic shapes. They can have a low-level cistern, the cistern can be close-coupled to the pan, or, best of all, it can be completely concealed.

When you are planning your new bathroom with all the pipes hidden behind a partition wall (see page 98, on planning) it is perfectly easy to lose cisterns for both lavatory and bidet therein as well. Several slim cisterns are available which will fit within a space only 6 in (150 mm) deep. If for some reason this is not feasible – or maybe you like to have your cistern in full view! – then there are space-saving cisterns made in a panel shape which have only a 4½ in (114 mm) projection and a neat top-press flush action. Excellent for the very small bathroom.

Most cisterns are operated by projecting levers, but there is an exceptionally neat push-lever which is almost flush. This is for use with concealed cisterns and can be fitted to the partition above the lavatory pan. It can also be fitted into the floor for foot operation, an excellent, hygienic but too little-used development.

Another hygienic device is the cantilevered lavatory. This is supported on its own steel cradle which is then concealed within that all-purpose partition wall. No need even to mount this on a structural wall, as it is the cradle rather than the wall which takes the weight. It is much easier to clean a bathroom floor – whether with a scrubbing brush or a vacuum cleaner – if you can swoop along beneath the various fittings rather than work round them.

The installation of a lavatory where there has not been one before is sometimes structurally difficult or extremely expensive because of the need to install large-bore discharge pipework to feed to the existing soil-stack. A device recently came on to the market which overcomes this problem, and I think it is worth mentioning here. This is a reasonably unobtrusive macerator which fixes to any horizontal outlet lavatory pan, operates electrically and need discharge into piping of no more than ¾ in diameter linking it with the soil-pipe. The difficult and expensive installation of

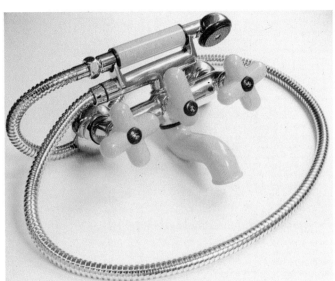

large-bore discharge pipework is thus avoided.

Lavatories, as you may have noticed, are getting lower and lower (only by the odd few millimetres, but still markedly lower). This is because current medical thinking favours the crouching position for the most efficient performance of the bodily functions. So whereas 16 in (405 mm) was the norm, the 15 in or 380 mm lavatory is now quite common. I thought you would like to know. 15 in seems rather low, especially for use by the standing male and higher models are still available if you prefer them. But maybe this is the time to promote the domestic urinal. It would make an admirable addition to the bathroom if there is room.

There are now many ranges of coloured taps. 1. is called Montmartre, and there are wash basin mixers, bidet mixers, stand-up and angled taps, as well as the bath set with hand-shower shown here. Other colours are red, yellow, blue and ivory, or there are nickel and polished brass finishes if you prefer. 2. A stylish range from Italy available also in red, blue, green and white epoxy resin finish. Kitchen taps are included in the range. 3. From left to right are shown lavatories with: a low-level cistern; a close-coupled cistern; and a concealed cistern. 4. and 5. There are brilliantly coloured lavatories to match most ranges. 4. is wall-hung, 5. is a close-coupled version from the same range. 6. This stainless steel lavatory, wash bowl and urinal were designed for industrial use but could look handsome in a high tech domestic setting. 7. If you want a lavatory where there is no convenient large-bore discharge pipe, this macerator fixed to any horizontal outlet lavatory could be the answer. It can evacuate waste matter up to 18 m (60 ft) away, or lift up to 1.8 m (6 ft).

4

5

6

7

Bidets

Like lavatories, bidets are made of vitreous china, and many manufacturers have bidets of similar design and height to their lavatories, including cantilevered models.

Quite rightly, bidet plumbing is subject to the strict Water Board rules and building regulations that apply to lavatories. This ensures there is no danger of flushing back which would be a health hazard. There must for instance be separate hot and cold water supply pipes, and drainage must be into a vented soil-pipe.

Most bidets have an ascending douche spray and a rim flush. However, there are also bidets which are filled from taps like a wash bowl, and as these do not have to conform to the rules I have mentioned, they are often useful in conversions where to do so would prove extremely difficult.

Taps for bidets are the same as those used for wash bowls and, with the same few exceptions, similarly badly designed and unattractive.

Showers

The section starting on page 109 is devoted to the whole subject of showers because for those trying to save energy and money they are preferable to baths, and so deserve a section to themselves.

The amount of water used in an average bath is much larger than that used in the average shower, although opinions vary as to the exact difference according to who is making the judgement. It follows then that every household should have at least one shower, and this can take the following forms:

1 A simple shower attachment at one end of the bath, with wall-mounted sockets or a slide bar enabling the handset to be fixed in a suitable position for easy use. This will have a curtain, or glass or plastic screen.
2 A shower cubicle, either specially built for its site or comprising one of the ready-made cubicles which are widely available. This will either have a fixed shower head or an adjustable handset as described above.
3 A small, tile-lined room complete with drainage, which acts as a shower room.

bathrooms of the land like wildfire (one firm which was early in the field has already ceased manufacturing its very respectable product), but they are worth considering, for they fill a real need. Perhaps too space-consuming for a small bathroom, they could be used to splendid effect in the conversion of a bigger room. Manufacturers' leaflets tend to show the whole room kitted out with their products, but a range of fittings along one or two walls would probably be more appropriate (and financially possible) in many homes.

Storage

Until quite recently, bathroom storage was limited to vanitory units (either specially made or the off-the-peg variety) and a few built-in cupboards. All that has changed in the last few years with the advent of built-in bathroom ranges consisting of modular units similar to those manufactured and marketed for kitchens.

These will conceal pipes, plumbing and uneven wall surfaces, though still providing for easy access in case of repairs. They act as sound-barriers between the bathroom and adjoining rooms. They provide storage cupboards – full-height, low-level and high-level – for all the impedimenta which gathers talc and fluff in many bathrooms, as well as for towels, bathrobes, spare soap, lavatory paper and other essentials. They case in the bath and wash bowl, incorporate wall panelling, work surfaces and shelving, and housing for dirty linen, as well as lavatory-roll holders, built-in mirrors and integral lighting. In addition to all this, they are available in either dark or light wood finishes, or in a variety of coloured laminated plastics.

These ranges have not exactly spread through the

1. and 2. show the two types of bidet. 1. is filled from taps just like a wash bowl and does not therefore have to conform to any Water Board regulations; 2. has lever control to rim or spray, and a pop-up waste. This does have to conform to Water Board regulations.

3. This is a particularly well-made vanitory unit with a broad marbled stone shelf and integral wash bowl over a painted wood cupboard. It measures 1325 × 800 × 560 mm (52$\frac{1}{5}$ × 31$\frac{1}{2}$ × 22 in). Similar units are available with twin bowls, or with single bowls set above a smaller cupboard.

4. This shows one of the ranges of fitted bathroom units now available. Constructed with wall panels to match the curve-fronted plastic units, it not only conceals pipes and damaged walls, but provides all the storage that could be required. Careful detailing includes inset handles, integral strip lighting and a special bracket system, which makes it possible for panels and units to be hung away from an uneven wall which might otherwise be difficult to deal with. There are various surface finishes, including simulated wood.

The ranges available are not so numerous that I can encourage you to be very selective in your purchase. But do aim for fittings which were palpably designed with the bathroom in mind and are not just a hasty adaptation of some firm's kitchen range (there are several of those about). Amongst other things, they should have the curved edges and corners which are more sympathetic to naked flesh, flush rather than projecting handles wherever possible, inset rather than projecting lavatory-roll holders, lighting and soap dishes, and a generally smooth and hygienic appearance.

There is no reason why the keen handyman should not fit out his own bathroom in this way, or why the more prosperous bathroom owner should not employ a designer and have it built for him. But the cost will be higher and the building works inevitably longer, dirtier and more tedious. Remember too that attractive details such as curved edges are not quite so easy to achieve on a one-off basis.

If your own bathroom is so small as to make the very idea of such elaborate equipage ludicrous, you are more likely to be in the market for a vanitory unit.

1. This vanitory unit has twin basins in an integral marbled stone shelf, set above dark-stained wood cupboards. Well-lit from above, the whole arrangement can be closed away behind dark-stained folding louvred doors in a well-organized bathroom/dressing room.

2. Architect Bernard Hunt has attractive storage arrangements in the large bathroom of his early Victorian house. Twin wash bowls are hung beneath a white marble surface and there are pine cupboards to take all the larger items which need to be kept in the bathroom. But the mirror above comes from an old chiffonier. Painted white, its small shelves make attractive repositories for pretty oddments. Despite its air of old-world charm, this bathroom has been very carefully designed. Note the slick way in which the taps are inserted into a marble upstand behind the wash bowls, and the high gloss of a well-lacquered board floor.

Vanitory units

Horrid though the name may be, and horrid though some of the ready-made units indeed are, the vanitory unit – which is basically a wash bowl set into a shelf, supported by a cupboard – can make all the difference between an untidy, uncomfortable little bathroom and a well-appointed and attractive one.

There are some decent ready-made units of standard height (about 780 mm) and depth (560 mm), but with usefully varying widths. Some are available wide enough to take two wash bowls rather than one, and all are available in various woods and different-coloured laminated plastics. Tops can be in plastic or wood, with inset bowls and there are also handsome marbled stone surfaces with integral bowls.

If the space you have to fill is awkward, if your requirements are very specific, or if you simply prefer something quite unique, a vanitory unit with bowl is a relatively easy piece of equipment to build-in, and then all the materials and colours could be exactly to your choice. You could have a Corian bowl and surface, or a marble or tiled surface with a coloured acrylic bowl mounted *under* the surface. You could have both surface and cupboard in wood, with a china or even stainless steel bowl. You are not then tied to the manufacturers' fairly limited range of materials and colours.

Free-standing storage

Some of the prettiest bathrooms are not a bit smooth or hygienic- and efficient-looking, but have free-standing furniture rather than the built-in variety just described. This is usually made of wood. Often it is stripped pine or, for a more masculine effect, dark mahogany. Free-standing furniture is generally chosen by those wanting to get away from the clinical bathroom look (of which more in Chapter 5 on decoration) and generally, though not always, is put into large bathrooms where there is space to accommodate it.

Old-fashioned washstands with deep cupboards and tiled tops are particularly appropriate for this purpose, so are chiffoniers which have a mirror and shelves above, a surface in which a wash bowl can be inserted, and storage cupboards below. But any wooden furniture intended for bathroom use should be treated with several coats of matt polyurethane varnish, otherwise the family splasher (and most families have one) will do it irreparable damage.

There is no reason why modern furniture should not be used in the same free-standing way, but it rarely is, except the cane and wicker variety which is perfectly at home in a damp atmosphere.

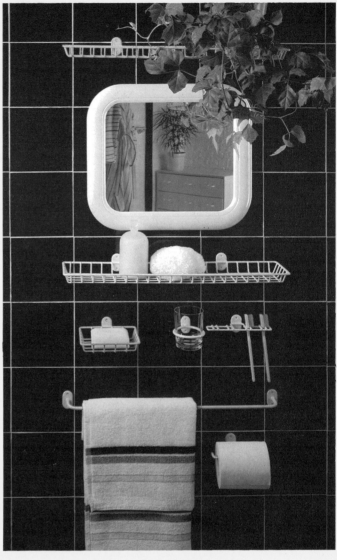

Accessories

Amongst accessories, I include towel rails, lavatory-roll holders, toothbrush holders, soap dishes and mirrors.

They are available for the most part in one of three materials; wood, plastic or chromed metal, and happily, although there is a lot of junk around, there is at least one good-looking range available in each.

The qualities to look for are simple clean lines, suitability for purpose and strength in use. After that, you choose the material suitable for your style of bathroom. Don't, for instance, buy homely wooden accessories for a slick, modern, all-plastic bathroom.

Be sure to have adequate accessories for your needs. There should be towel rails near the shower, the bath and the wash bowl unless you want to drip water over the floor, though sometimes if the sanitaryware is adjacent, one towel rail can double for two uses, and a small ring holder will generally be sufficient for the wash bowl. At least one rail should be heated or be in close proximity to a central heating outlet.

Soap dishes are a dubious extra. Soap recesses to the wash bowl can avoid the necessity of having one there. Over the bath, shower and bidet, the ideal arrangement – better than a dangerous projecting affair – is a dish set into the wall, and many tile manufacturers offer these in sizes and colours to complement their tile ranges.

Toothbrush holders tend to be rickety, projecting contraptions. There are handsome, solid ones though, especially amongst the very well-designed plastic and wooden ranges. Whichever you choose, be sure there are sufficient mugs and brush holders for the number of people using the bathroom. Lavatory-roll holders are in similar styles, but their positioning is important. I became particularly aware of this when suffering from a badly damaged shoulder and went through contortionist agonies getting at the paper in some people's bathrooms. To one side of the lavatory and at low level is best, *not* behind it and way above your head.

3

Choose accessories to match your style of bathroom. 1. is a new range which combines white vitreous china with dark-stained wood in a way which would be most appropriate for a very masculine bathroom or even one with period aspirations. Everything is solid and sturdy, very different from the delicate-looking plastic-covered wire range shown in 2. Available in red or white, this is in fact perfectly strong, unbelievably inexpensive, and with its bright good looks would suit young people setting up home for the first time who are perhaps not eager to invest in more costly accessories. 3. This well-designed ABS plastic range has now been on the market for some time, though it still looks very fresh and modern, especially in its most recent colours: navy and red. Relatively inexpensive, it includes coordinating shelves, toothbrush and mug holders, towel rings, bath racks, towel rails, mirrors and soap dishes – in fact everything you could possibly want for bathroom use.

4. Fix your lavatory-roll holder where you can easily reach it when you are sitting on the loo – not up behind your left shoulder, or feet away on the back of the door.

4

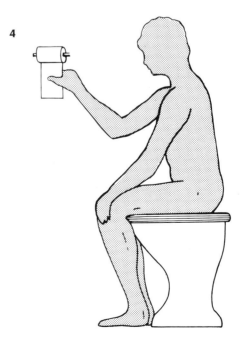

Planning

Bathrooms are often small rooms. Not all, of course. Some people can revel in the luxurious space of a room in an old house which has been converted to make a bathroom, and there is even the occasional modern house or flat where an unwonted amount of square footage has been lavished on the bathroom. But generally, they come last in pecking order when space is being allocated, and quite often they are tiny to the point of pokiness.

They should, therefore, be extremely carefully planned to make the best possible use of the area which *is* available, not only from a visual and comfort point of view, but also so that plumbing, which is expensive like all specialist trades, can be done as economically as possible.

Two types of job are likely to be tackled. First, there is the conversion or updating of an existing bathroom. Second, the building of an extension to make a new bathroom, or the conversion of another room in the house into a bathroom. In either case, take note of the recommendations concerning building regulations and planning approval contained in the introductory section of this book (page 13), to see when they are applicable.

Replanning an existing bathroom

This type of room probably needs the most careful consideration before you start work. To begin with, what in the way of existing equipment should you keep, and what abandon? Think long and hard if what you are about to pull apart is a real period bathroom, complete with huge bath, wide wash bowl and old-fashioned taps. Do not heave them out with reckless abandon, for you will never see their like again. And unless they are cracked and chipped beyond repair, the bath can probably be resurfaced and the taps rechromed or, if they are brass, buffed up. It may be that all that is really necessary is a paint and paper job, boosted by new tiles and flooring. And even the most ordinary little bathroom, a slot with plain equipment but where there is no need (or perhaps money) for total reorganization, can be pleasantly updated using much of the existing equipment but with the addition of new taps and accessories, paint and possibly a smart new vanitory unit and bowl. In other words, consider your assets well before deciding to dispense with them regardless.

Painter Chloe Cheese lives in a great studio flat in a converted Bermondsey warehouse, with only the bathroom separated from the rest of the space. In this room which is lined with white tiles, the bath is raised, the shower tray simply a lowered section of the floor, and the pink blind hides a view over a main railway line.

Rearranging the plumbing

It may be, though, that what you have in mind, indeed what your existing bathroom desperately needs, is some radical alteration, perhaps involving entirely new equipment. This is when you will want to investigate the existing plumbing and pipe runs in order to assess the possibilities. Anything is *possible*. If existing water pipes enter the room at one side but you would like to move the bath and wash bowl to the other, you can do so by running the pipes under the floor to emerge in their new position, provided you arrange an adequate drop to ensure the easy flow of water. But it will take time and cost money, so weigh up the merits of such a job first. Likewise, the soil-pipe for the lavatory which will probably be connected to an outside wall will be expensive to move more than a short distance.

What you can do perfectly feasibly – in addition of course to replacing obsolete or ugly sanitaryware – is to move things within the range of the existing plumbing outlets so that the whole room functions that much better. For instance, a bath running along one wall which has a door in it may be very much more comfortable to use running along another which doesn't – and it can be moved with very little extension of the water pipes, as shown.

Or it may be that a wash basin is set in just the position on a wall which precludes it being built into a vanitory unit because of a door opening, whereas moving it just two feet along would get rid of this obstacle, as shown.

Minor but vital alterations of this nature can make a considerable difference to the comfort of a room.

Size variations

There is little point in going into long descriptions of the size ranges of the different pieces of equipment, for the variations are considerable and whatever your requirement you will almost certainly find something to fit it. Remember, too, that replacing bulky sanitaryware with streamlined pieces of smaller dimensions will not only make the room look bigger, but will release a gratifying amount of actual space.

Here is a rough guide to some of the main dimensions. A bath can be as small as 3 ft 6 in in length (1050 mm), but this is the sitz two-level bath in which you sit upright and will not appeal to those who like to recline full-length. More conventional models vary in length from 4 ft 6 in (1370 mm) to 6 ft (1828 mm), but in addition there are wedge-shaped baths to fit into a corner, circular ones to set in the centre of a large room, and others as mentioned on page 85. Wash bowls too vary enormously in both inner and outer dimensions, and the differing shapes which manufacturers have contrived for this simple artefact can only be regarded with awe and admiration. There are some, really only suitable for handwashing in a cloakroom, which project no more than 6 in (152 mm) into the room, part of the bowl being recessed into the wall, whilst other luxurious models with wide surrounds project as much as 23 in (590 mm); with

every conceivable shape and dimension in between. Shower trays start at a minimum 30 in (750 mm) square, but there are many larger ones, and one particularly spacious ready-made circular shower compartment which is 6 ft 6 in (2 m) in diameter.

It is worth mentioning here a device which has immensely glamorous connotations. This is the sunken bath. Now this bath has to have somewhere to sink to, and in most modern houses it cannot be considered unless you build a dais and sink it into that. But in older houses with high rooms, or possibly in a new and specially designed extension, there may be room within the interfloor space. You will need something like 2 ft (609 mm) to accommodate the underside of the bath, but if you are building a false lowered ceiling into a very high room below, this could work well. One architect of impeccably tidy habits, irritated by the scales which cluttered her bathroom, sank those into the floor too.

They looked very appealing emerging from the closely carpeted floor.

Scale drawing
It is a good idea when you are replanning your room to make a scale drawing of the size and shape available. Cut out shapes of the equipment you want to fit in and work out in this basic way whether it is all feasible. Several manufacturers' brochures contain scale cut-outs of their wares, which is a help. You may find that the shower tray or bidet you had coveted but thought too bulky *will* just go in or, sadly, that it won't. But this scaled-down paperwork will give you irrefutable evidence one way or the other.

Concealing the pipes
When you are replanning the room, consider also the visual implications of what you are doing. It may be that

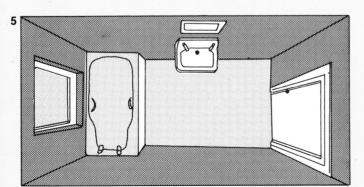

1. and 2. Turn the bath through an angle of 45° so that it is no longer close to the door.

3. and 4. Moving the wash bowl away from the door means it can be built into a vanitory unit, thus concealing plumbing, providing a shelf all round and making storage for bathroom paraphernalia.

5. The sitz two-level bath may not be to everybody's taste, but since it is only 1050 mm (42 in) long, it will enable a tiny slot of a room to be used as a bathroom.

the place was festooned with pipes when you started and that you are adding one or two more. Possibly you like that effect? I once saw a bathroom in a rented flat where the occupants were not prepared to spend too much money on remedial work and they had simply turned adversity to advantage by painting the liberal quantity of pipes with which that bathroom was endowed in a profusion of brilliant colours. Fun, but not everyone's choice. Pipes collect dirt, they need to be decorated each time the room is, and in most cases are best hidden.

Work out your methods at the planning stage. Pipes can be concealed behind built-in cupboards and certainly within one of the systems of built-in units mentioned in the previous chapter. Horizontal pipes can be boxed in and the resulting protrusion form seating if it is at low level, or a shelf if it is at waist height. Vertical pipes can be lost within a full-height cupboard. Or it is sometimes simpler to make a timber stud and plaster-board partition wall which screens off the whole of one side of a room with its disfiguring pipes and the lavatory cistern. A depth of 6 in (150 mm) is generally sufficient, certainly if one of the special slimline cisterns is used.

If you have inherited the pipes you may need ingenuity and effort to lose them, but if the planning is your own, ensure that you have as few as possible contained as closely as possible, and then your problems will be diminished.

Here are some examples of the ways in which various pipes likely to be found in a bathroom can be enclosed.

A new bathroom

If the job you have in mind is a completely new bathroom, albeit a small one, you are not nearly so constrained by existing facilities, though again you must consider with the help of a scale drawing the sizes of the various pieces of equipment you want to get in. And again it will be wise to have the various items sited as close as possible to the water sources. If a new extension is in question, you, or your architect, will have considered this matter from the start and sited the extension accordingly – above the kitchen or backing on to another bathroom, for instance, so that their plumbing facilities can be shared. But if you are going to transform a room that was previously a bedroom, ensure that it is one not too far away from the house's existing plumbing – unless, that is, expense and inconvenience do not concern you. Then plan your room, particularly if it is a large one where you might be tempted to do otherwise, so that the plumbing outlets for bath, shower, lavatory, bidet and wash bowl are grouped fairly closely together.

If you are tempted to have the bath taps on one wall, the bidet taps on another and the wash bowl taps on a third – to take an extreme case of bad planning – your plumbing costs will reflect your carelessness.

Pipe concealment will follow the same general principles as in the refurbished bathroom, though it is to be hoped that the job will be made easier by your

Make use of the space which houses the pipes. In 1. the partition which conceals pipes to the lavatory and bidet has a useful waist-height shelf running across the top. In 2. there is a high cupboard with mirror-faced sliding doors and a recessed shelf, all arranged within the partitioning which conceals pipes around the wash bowl.

3. Designer John McConnell has all his sanitaryware ranged along one wall of his large bathroom (apart from the shower, see page 114), and the plumbing is concealed behind a shoulder-height partition with shelf above. Lights are fixed to this shelf, and their wiring too is carried away behind the partition. Note the elegantly glazed Edwardian screen which shields bathers from draughts, and the boxed-in bath with tiled sides. This room is stunning in its simplicity, and any hint of coldness is banished by very adequate central heating.

thoughtful disposition of the plumbing. The partition wall may be used to great effect here, detracting little in terms of space and containing everything you wish to conceal. Other expedients should be carefully exploited so that they contribute to the overall appearance and orderliness of the room as well as performing their concealing function. A vanitory unit set across one wall to hide pipework, for instance, should be well-designed, strongly made and fully equipped with storage shelves; and there should be no awkward gaps, cracks or spaces between it and the walls where dust can gather. In other words, don't just box the pipes in, but ensure that the boxing contributes in some way to the aesthetic and function of the room.

Things to remember

Whether your room is a new or refurbished one, and even if it is small, try to incorporate those features which so many bathrooms lack and which can make all the difference in terms of comfort, tidiness and cleanliness. *Storage* has been mentioned, and this will vary in extent according to the size of your bathroom, your family and your possessions, but do not underestimate your requirements if you like an orderly style of life. A *dirty-linen box* should also form part of the equipment and a built-in one would be infinitely preferable to the baskets and plastic bins which the shops offer us. Most of the ranges of ready-made bathroom units incorporate such a fitting, but it is possible to build your own into a newly designed bathroom. The low-level trunking to conceal pipes which has been turned into a seat, mentioned on page 102, could have a flap which lifts up to reveal a clothes bin, or a range of built-in cupboards could have a hinge-down flap opening for the same purpose. A bath often takes up only part of a length of wall. The remaining space up to the corner could be boxed in to form a bin. The possibilities are numerous and not difficult to contrive.

Shelf space

Another facility you will want to incorporate is adequate shelf area around the wash bowl, or twin wash bowls. Vanitory units have been mentioned and they provide exactly the sort of flat surface people want and on which they can put hand cream, aftershave lotion, face tissues and so on, and wrist-watches and rings whilst they wash their hands. It may be, though, that there simply is not the space for such an arrangement around the bowl. Apart from installing a basin which has as wide a rim as possible (and some have virtually none), arrange to have a broad and safe shelf above the bowl or even at lower level — perhaps an extension of the boxing-in which conceals pipes. A shelf there must certainly be if washtime frustrations are to be avoided.

A mirror

Make sure an adequate-sized mirror is included in your plan. Too much mirror glass in a bathroom, despite its glittering appeal, can be an early morning depressant to

4

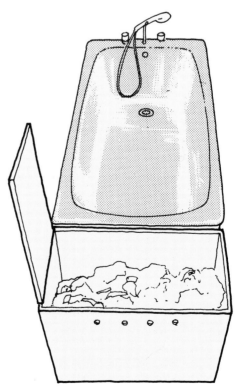

5

1. and 2. are exceptionally small basins which may be fitted into spaces you thought were hopelessly inadequate. They are suitable for hand-rinsing rather than large-scale washing. 1. is called Barbican and projects only 15 cm (6 in) into the room, as well as having an integral lavatory roll holder. 2. has an overall measurement of only 260 × 360 mm ($10\frac{1}{5} \times 14\frac{1}{5}$ in), which is also considerably smaller than most basins.

3. is a wall-hung basin of particularly simple and appealing design. It comes in three sizes, the largest being 600 × 450 mm ($23\frac{3}{5} \times 17\frac{3}{4}$ in), and can be supplied with or without tapholes (the latter being an excellent option since it means the taps may be wall fixed).

4. Mirrors have their disadvantages. They may show more than you want to see, damp air condenses on their surface, and they show every soap splash. But in this particularly glamorous bathroom, in a house with first-rate central heating and adequate domestic help, none of these difficulties applies. Beautifully cloud-shaped mirrors are fixed to the doors of all the built-in cupboards and dramatize the bath as well as doubling the apparent size of an already huge room.

5. Don't waste the space between the end of the bath and the wall, especially if you only have a small room. Build in a dirty linen box. Its lift-up top can be covered with cork tiles and it will then double as a stool.

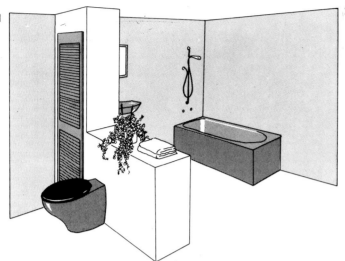

the less-than-slender, besides encouraging a tendency to condensation (see Chapter 4), but an inadequate mirror is infuriating when you are shaving, inspecting the progress of wrinkles or painting your eyelids. A large one over the wash bowl can be placed at a height to suit the principal users, but not so low as to attract every splash from spluttering tooth-brushers. A more expensive, but generally satisfactory arrangement, is to have a shallow storage cupboard above the bowl, with sliding doors faced in mirror glass. Sometimes it is possible to conceal lights behind the doors, so that this one fitting effectively fulfills three functions.

Privacy

This is the time to think about a measure of privacy in the bathroom, certainly in the family bathroom which may need to be used by several children at once. If the bathroom contains a lavatory and is large enough, partial screening of the lavatory by a waist-height partition wall will give at least an illusion of visual privacy, and this wall could also incorporate storage cupboards. A separate shower cabinet could be arranged behind a full-height partition wall where there is sufficient room.

A seat

Every bathroom should have a seat of some sort. You may be the type of person who likes to retreat to the bathroom and read the newspaper in peace and comfort, and if yours is a large bathroom, a chaise-

1. In a reasonably sized family bathroom it makes sense to screen the lavatory so that more than one person – particularly children – can use the room at the same time. Here, screening and storage are combined. 2. Setting the wash-bowl into a broad shelf provides space for all the paraphernalia which goes with washing. In this room the shelf is carried on across a window wall to conceal plumbing pipes, and is tiled for easy cleaning.

Edwardian wooden towel rails provided plenty of hanging space, and are having a well-deserved revival in popularity. Both pine and darkwood models (as seen here) are available. Be sure the one you choose is stable on its feet – some wobble and collapse when laden with towels.

longue – perhaps made of cane with towelling-covered cushions – can be provided for you. But even if the room is of a less lavish order and you just want to perch for a few moments whilst you cut your toe-nails, this should be possible. Mention has already been made of low-level boxing-in used to form a seat. Another could be contrived from wooden slats along part of a wall, perhaps bridging a gap between other fixtures, and a bench seat could also be made if there is space at one end of the bath.

Medicine cupboard

There should be a separate and lockable medicine cupboard. Do *not*, for safety reasons, have your medicines shoved into a corner of the general storage cupboard. If there are small children in the family, the cupboard should ideally be at a high level, out of their reach.

Towel rails

Every bathroom needs at least one towel rail, and its situation should be thought about during the initial planning stages. Do not make the mistake of putting it (or them) more than an arm's length away from where it will be used. If you have ever, in an unfamiliar bathroom, groped for a non-existent towel with soap in your eyes and dripping hands, you will know what I mean. So have one towel rail near the wash bowl and – if they are not immediately adjacent – one near the bath and shower. If possible, towel rails should also be near a heat source such as a radiator or warm air outlet, so that the towels dry quickly. Heated towel rails (usually oil-filled) perform this function satisfactorily, and often provide the only form of heating in a very small bathroom. Other possibilities are an old-fashioned, free-standing wooden rail, a wooden pole mounted the length of one wall, or wall-mounted rings.

With all the planning done on paper beforehand, the likelihood of bad errors in the arrangement of your bathroom is much reduced. You will not end up with a wash bowl which is so large it dominates a tiny space, or with a bidet so tightly squeezed in it is impossible to use.

Showers

Consider the advantages of showers:

1. They need take up far less room than a bath.
2. They use considerably less hot water.
3. Therefore they are cheaper to use.
4. Taking a shower, you rinse the dirt away, rather than wallow in it.
5. A small shower compartment would be cheaper to install than a bath, and certainly much cheaper than a complete bathroom.
6. A shower is quicker to use.
7. It is also safer to use, especially if the shower tray has a non-slip surface.

Despite all this, many people, especially women and including me, cling to their grimy wallow. The reasons are historic rather than valid. Firstly, too many British bathrooms were for too long inadequately heated, so it was infinitely preferable to get into a deep hot bath rather than stand in a tepid trickle. Which brings me to

1. and 2. Instantaneous electric showers are economical to use – the water is only heated as and when you need it – and may be installed without extensive and expensive new plumbing. Many of them are also rather well designed, including the two shown here. Both have slide bar fixings for the handset, and automatic temperature stabilizers.

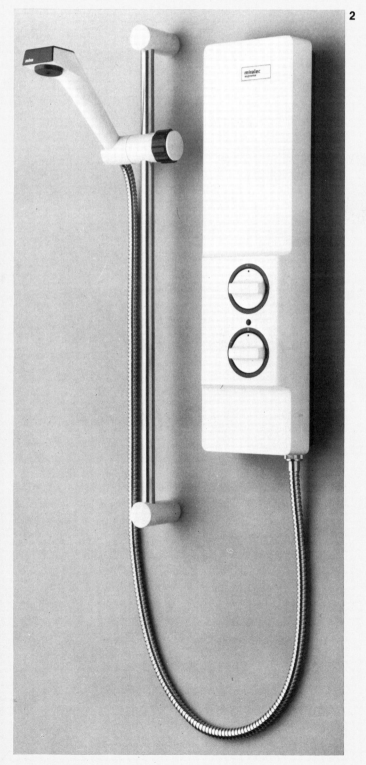

the second reason. Anyone who has ever taken a shower in the United States will appreciate the difference between the great whoosh of water which descends on you there and the feeble flow from most British showers. The water pressure in this country is notoriously low.

However, not only are far more bathrooms now adequately heated, but technical developments mean that it is possible to have a much more powerful shower. In addition, there are efficient, thermostatically controlled mixers to avoid the alternative scalding and freezing douches which were once such a feature. They can also ensure that the water keeps on flowing whatever else happens in the house, unlike the shower controls which my husband was unfortunate enough to encounter in one Italian holiday hotel. Having soaped himself energetically all over, he turned on the shower intending to have a rinse down. But nothing happened – for nearly three-quarters of an hour – as the other guests were already tapping the water supply. Not a pleasant experience.

There are various general points to remember when planning a shower, apart from the specific ones which apply to each type of shower.

1 The water outlets should be adjustable to suit the needs of various-sized users. A fixed shower head can simply be hinged so that its direction is changed as required, or the hose and handset type can move up and down a slide bar, or the handset can be plugged into wall-mounted sockets at various heights.

2 The control should be near the entrance to the shower cubicle, so that the water pressure and temperature can be pre-set from outside. This simple arrangement – not common in the showers I have encountered – would win over to showering many people who are too impatient, inept or nervous to fiddle about with the controls while waiting for the water to hit them.

3 Although it is possible to have a shower compartment as small as 30 × 30 in (750 mm), and this is certainly better than not having one at all, a considerably bigger one is better, for a large person could not bend over to pick up the soap very easily in a space 30 in square.

4 A seat is a splendid addition, particularly for elderly people, and the shower head should be arranged so that it can be directed over the seat.

Plumbing arrangements

Like every other piece of bathroom equipment, a shower should be installed as closely as possible to existing water supplies for cheapness and ease of installation.

As I said before, water pressures are generally low in this country, hence the type of showers which make our American friends laugh or wail with frustration. But the greatest head of pressure is achieved by having a good distance between the bottom of the cold water storage cistern (feeding a separate hot water supply) and the shower outlet. If the distance is less than 3 ft (915 mm), which is not uncommon in a flat or bungalow, you can employ one of two remedies. Either move the tank to a higher position, or if that is not possible, install a pump to boost the pressure.

Heaters which are plumbed directly to the cold water mains can also be used to overcome the problem. No pump or expensive resiting of the cold water tank is necessary to get adequate pressure with the correct type of instant heater. In addition, they are economical since the water is only heated as and when it is needed.

Assuming you have taken care of the plumbing arrangements, your shower can be one of three types:

Over the bath

This is the simplest type of shower to arrange, because its plumbing will be incorporated in the bath plumbing. The only drawback is that it provides no real *extra* facility, as, while the bath is being used for its prime function, it can hardly be used for showering at the same time. All the same, it is useful for the family where some like to shower, some to bath – and for hair-washing. The bath over which the shower is installed should for reasons of comfort be as large as possible, and for reasons of safety it should have a non-slip bottom.

To keep the occupant from spraying the whole room, a screen will be necessary. The cheapest is a plastic curtain, though as even the best quickly become stained and unpleasant-looking, a fixed screen is better. There are anodized aluminium frames with either sliding, folding or hinged doors, and plastic or glass panels *can*

Designers Tony and Anne Barnes planned and largely built this bathroom themselves. An advantage of acrylic baths is their lightness, which makes them easily transportable. This particular shape of bath is ideal to use with a wall-mounted shower, and there is no need for a shower curtain to prevent splashing on the long-haired white carpet. Tiled walls make the arrangement perfectly practical.

be arranged so that they virtually encase the bath, but this must make a pretty claustrophobic little enclosure for the sit-down bather, and it would be better to have a partial screen of the hinged or folding type, with see-through or smoked-glass panels.

Separate shower compartment

The separate shower compartment is of much more general use. It can be simply a ready-made shower cubicle, similar in construction to the screens used around the bath. Or it may be a stove-enamelled steel or plastic compartment with a curtained opening. These, unfortunately, are generally in crude pastel colours and similarly awful design. But as always there are exceptions, including some sparklingly elegant models imported from Italy. The more expensive of these Italian jobs are free-standing and circular. They come in several sizes and degrees of elaboration (with integral shower rails, shelves, lighting and soap trays, for instance) and are really only suitable for the large-scale room. A cheaper and much more conventional compartment is imported from Italy by the same company. It is square, but equally handsome, and has a moulded plastic seat.

The ideal bathroom shower compartment will probably be custom-built, and if you are planning a whole new bathroom it should be possible to wall off a segment of the room for this purpose. Most economically, it will be in a corner where two walls meet so that only one side needs to be built up, the fourth being used as an entrance. This newly built wall can be of brick or concrete blocks, or it can be a simple timber frame and plasterboard construction. The shower side of the wall will have a waterproof lining, the outer side will be decorated to suit the general scheme of the bathroom. The shower tray itself can be a proprietary one or, if your requirements are specific and unusual, you can build and tile your own. A really large compartment of this sort will not even need a curtain or door.

Shower compartment outside the bathroom

The joy of a shower compartment is that, bearing in mind the need for economical plumbing, it can be sited in all sorts of tight corners where a full-scale bathroom would be out of the question. It can be in the bedroom, where it is of far more use than the ubiquitous wash bowl. Built into a range of storage cupboards, it need not even proclaim its presence when doors are shut, and though it will quite probably not be deep enough to allow the user to dry and dress before emerging, it can probably have extra width for the purpose.

Another useful place to have a shower is near the

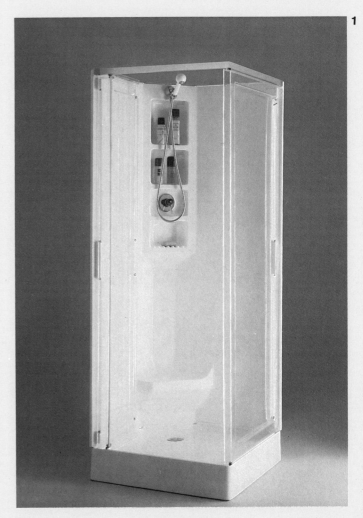

garden door, especially when the household includes children, gardeners and handymen. There is more likely to be unused space which can be incorporated for this purpose in older houses (sculleries, tool cupboards, outside lavatories, or in an existing cloakroom or laundry room), though in newer properties a small extension to hold a shower would be a relatively simple proposition. This type of shower would ease the pressure on a one-bathroom house, as children could shower there on coming in from the garden, and have no need for a bath before bedtime.

If there is not much space in your home, the shower room can be a surrogate bathroom, having wash bowl and lavatory as well as the actual shower. With the increasing emphasis on provision of single-person dwellings as well as the interest in saving energy by showering instead of bathing, I predict that this type of room will become more and more common. A small bedroom might even be turned into twin shower rooms, with the plumbing back-to-back. The cupboard under the stairs is large enough to make a shower room in some houses, or the wasted space at the end of a

2

3

Most of the free-standing shower cabinets on the market are depressingly unattractive, with these two cabinets of Italian manufacture being amongst the very few exceptions. 1. The Antares is made of acrylic, with clear fold-back doors, and is of a conventional shape, 750 mm (30 in) square, but with an integral stool and a shelf for soaps, shampoos and lotions. There is a sensible anti-slip floor and its manufacturers claim the whole cabinet is easily assembled within half an hour using only six screws.

2. *Doccia tonda* means 'round shower' and is from the Aquarius range. Of similar design and construction to the square shower, its base is designed to be free standing and there is a warm-water pipe on which to hang towels. It has a sliding, clear acrylic door, and both the base and back panel come in various colours including red, blue, black and moss-green. There is a larger version of similar design, and yes, all these showers are extremely expensive, partly because they are imported.

3. The shower in Chloe Cheese's bathroom is simply a recess in the white-tiled platform which contains her bath. Walls and floor are all tiled, so there is no need for shower curtains. In fact any possible way to avoid shower curtains – a large, deep shower tray or an arrangement such as this – should be adopted, for I haven't found one yet which does not quickly deteriorate into a stained and unappealing mess.

landing or corridor. A fresh look at your own home could be revealing.

Though a separate shower room of this nature can be planned and equipped in a conventional way, some extra thought may well turn it into a more unusual place.

The whole room could, for instance, be tiled, including the floor, and with self-drainage become a complete shower compartment. The one shown here is large, so there is room for a bath too (as well as a singular view over the railway lines when the Venetian blinds are raised), but this is just an agreeable addition. The room, which has its own separate lavatory and wash bowl, would have been almost as practical with just the integral shower.

In open shower rooms, it is even more important than in a normal shower compartment that the tiling should be precise and accurate – for mistakes will glare at you – and completely sealed against water. The shower area will (need I point out) be set well away from the door, which will nevertheless best be painted in a good hard gloss paint or, if it is hardwood, treated with a matt seal from which the odd droplet of water can easily be wiped.

1

Shower controls

These come in varying degrees of sophistication which, not unnaturally, are reflected in the price.

On a bath, it is usual to have a dual-flow handset attachment, operated by the same taps which produce the bath water. The flow is diverted from one to the other by a lever, and the best attachments are those which automatically revert to 'bath' when the water is turned off, otherwise you are likely to get an unexpected deluge if the lever is inadvertently left in the 'shower' position.

Get as simple a model as possible, for the reasons explained in the section on taps. Individual wall-fixed sockets, or sliding rails, are used to hold the handset when the shower is being operated.

A variety of arrangements are available when the shower is separate from the bath. The most sophisticated include both thermostatic control and flow control, with absolutely no danger of the temperature changing markedly if a tap is turned on elsewhere in the house. This seems to me an essential rather than a luxury if the shower is to be used by elderly people or children, and one for which it is well worth paying extra. However, in a one- or two-person home the hazards will obviously diminish. The controls may be surface mounted or inset, and the latter arrangement naturally contributes more to a smooth streamlined look. Shower outlets can be built in and fixed, with a swivelling head, or have a handset arrangement similar to the type used on a bath.

Less sophisticated controls enable you to manipulate flow and temperature independently, but there is no thermostatic control, and the most basic sort are little more than mixers, with the pressure being affected each time you alter the temperature control and vice versa.

Finishes on all these shower controls are generally chrome or plastic, but gold-plated models are available.

1. John McConnell built this simple but large shower compartment in his own bathroom, incorporating a standard ceramic shower tray, and lined the whole thing, inside and out, with white tiles for easy cleaning. A plastic-covered wire basket hangs on the wall to hold shampoo, sponge, etc. and the shower is of the traditional overhead rather than the wall-mounted variety. Note the hooks for bathrobes or towels which are conveniently fixed to either side of the entrance.

2. shows, left, an extremely neat arrangement: a built-in shower control (not thermostatic) with entirely concealed plumbing and fixed shower head which can be directed at various angles. Right is a similar shower control, but this time it is surface-mounted, the stainless steel pipework is exposed and there is a similar shower head. Note that the built-in version requires a 75-mm (3-in) depth of concealment in the wall – and its installation can be a messy business if you are dealing with existing plaster or a ready-tiled wall.

3. shows, right, a fully thermostatic shower control. Designed specifically for flush fitting and for connection to concealed pipework, it is described as thermoscopic by its makers, and an elliptical plate hides all but the numbered temperature control and the separate flow control. For people who find the more usual mounting of both these controls on one knob confusing in moments of stress, this separation will be a welcome innovation.

4. This is the larger version of the Aquarius shower cabinet shown on page 113. It is perfectly suitable for bathing as well as showering and has a seat built into its deep tray. It can be supplied with built-in whirlpool jets, ideal, say the manufacturers, for relieving tension. It would certainly make a luxurious bath/shower cabinet in a bathroom of reasonable size – at a price.

2

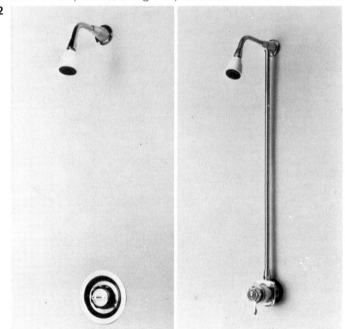

3

4

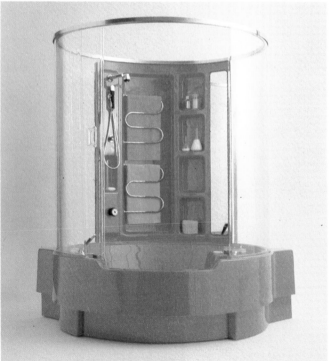

Technicalities

My earliest memories are of a freezing bathroom which ran with condensation every time someone took a bath. Even as a child I spent as little time there as possible. My mother certainly did not put on her make-up there, and she would have been hard pressed if she had tried, for there was only a tiny mirror, a hanging pendant light which cast an ugly glow at night and one small frosted glass window which did little better during the day. A big and noisy gas appliance provided hot water, and such warmth as there was. We were not particularly poor and nor, I might add, was this so very long ago.

Few people are likely to endure this sort of purgatory now. More fool them if they do because it is relatively simple and not desperately expensive to make a bathroom which is warm, well-lit and does not suffer from condensation problems.

Heating

Many bathrooms will benefit from whole-house central heating, having either a radiator or a warm air outlet. Fine. The only necessary addition is an oil-filled electrically heated radiator (another feature of that childhood bathroom was dank, cold towels). This will both dry towels and take the chill off on those mid-season days when the central heating is off and when a totally unheated room is not quite comfortable for stripping down to the buff.

Supposing, though, that the house is not centrally heated. You certainly cannot have an electric fire in a bathroom, or even a 3-amp plug. But a convector heater is both safe and supplies a very desirable instant heat. Don't just plonk it on the wall where the fancy takes you. Build it in unobtrusively with other fittings so that it contributes to the general design of the room. Both gas and electric models are available, but since gas models have to be sited on an outside wall to allow for the intake and discharge of air, an electric type will often prove to be more convenient.

Electric infra-red heaters, set out of the reach of children and with obligatory pull-cord switches, are another possibility and they certainly provide a quick blast of heat for the duration of a shower or bath. What they do *not* do is heat all the room surfaces instantly – cold mirrors, tiles, window glass, etc. – and so they do very little to prevent condensation.

Something to avoid in bathrooms more than anywhere else is ill-fitting doors and windows, unless you want pleasant warmth to be spoilt by freezing draughts. If there are gaps, do some remedial work with self-adhesive rubber or plastic-foam draught stripping.

Hot water

The pleasures of hot water are much underestimated. One of the minor delights of life is to sit in it – or, if you must, stand under it – either relaxing in a mindless sort of way, or planning the day's work. Lovely, if expensive, and for me a much greater comfort than either food or drink.

But the water *must* be hot. In many bathrooms water will be heated by the same means as the space heating, i.e. a gas, solid fuel or oil-fired boiler. In addition there will be an immersion heater if the boiler does not cope with the water independently when the space heating is turned off. It is in any case very often cheaper to heat the water by this means when space heating is not required.

Or it may be that water is always heated by an immersion heater and is totally independent of the space heating system. But in either case make sure there is sufficient capacity to provide really hot water at all times. If you are number four in the family, taking a bath when the system is really only up to coping with three, then one of life's little pleasures disappears in a lot of tepid water. So be advised by a heating engineer or the suppliers who are installing the heating system, and get the largest boiler or immersion heater they recommend.

If there is no central heating or immersion heater, or if the existing ones are not of sufficient capacity to serve the additional bathroom you may be planning, the alternatives are:

1 To put in a new boiler of larger capacity. This may be a good plan anyway if you own a house with an antiquated appliance.

2 To have an additional, independent water heater. If this is to heat water simply for a shower and wash bowl, an electric storage heater will be adequate, and there are some neat and well-designed models which do nothing to mar the appearance of a painstakingly planned room. But, if a full bathroom, complete with bath, is being planned, a gas instantaneous heater will be necessary to cope with the demand for large quantities of water. This type of multipoint-outlet heater is essential if the water is to supply the kitchen as well. Simple, pleasant designs are available and the heater can be situated in a cupboard or elsewhere out of sight if you prefer, but the cupboard must be

1. Even if your home is not centrally heated, be sure to have a warm bathroom. This is not only pleasant for comfortable bathing, but essential if you want there to be no danger of condensation. An electrical convector heater is a good source of heat, and a neat idea would be to conceal it within the same cavity which conceals plumbing pipes, and then operate it from a pull-cord near the door. Safe and unobtrusive, it will make an excellent substitute for genuine central heating.

2. This bathroom is centrally heated, but it is a small room, and as wall space was at a premium the radiator was mounted vertically to take up as little space as possible. Towel rings above mean there are always warm dry towels. Note too the 'warm' treatment of this room: practically every surface, including the ceiling, is covered in cork tiles and the paintwork (radiator too) is bright red. The cork surfaces would be an excellent condensation-deterrent, if this were necessary.

1. **Architects Vernoique and David Richmond cleverly contrived a shower/cloakroom in a small space off the living area in their basement flat. Artificial light comes from lamps set around the tilting mirror over their wash bowl, and glass bricks in one wall enable daylight to be 'borrowed' from the living area beyond. Note how the shape of the tiled surface behind the wash bowl echoes the shape of the tiled wall surface. It is details like this which give great style to even very small rooms.**

2. **Designer Andrew Holmes's bathroom, despite being in a London house, is not particularly overlooked. He liked the feeling of having a room flooded with light (the effect doubled by a judiciously placed mirror), and didn't want the clear shape cluttered by curtains. So he hung a simple white blind to be pulled down at night. Note the long, white-tiled shelf which contains a wash bowl, and the chromed tubular steel pole running beneath it to form a particularly spacious towel rail.**

ventilated and usually an outside flue will be necessary.

Whatever your water heating system, short pipe-runs and a thermostatic control on the source, set at the average of 150°F (65°C), will help in the drive to conserve energy, and when there is a stored supply of water the hot tank should be well lagged.

Lighting

Although poor lighting in a bathroom is not so potentially hazardous as poor lighting in a kitchen, it does cast an indefinable aura of gloom over the place, as well as making activities such as applying make-up and reading the bathroom scales both tedious and difficult. This is a room where low lighting is quite out of place, however glamorous and relaxing an atmosphere you are aiming to create, and if you can fill the room with sunshine as well as artificial light, so much the better.

If you are making a bathroom from scratch – either building an extension or converting a space which was previously used for something entirely different – it will be easier to contrive an east- or west-facing window than if you are refurbishing an existing bathroom. And east- or west-facing windows mean sunny baths either early in the morning or early in the evening, both of them great life-enhancers. But wherever your window, make it large enough to give ample light to all parts of the room, whilst not being so large as to discharge heat at a formidable pace on cold days; unless you are going to indulge in double-glazing which will reduce heat-loss a little.

One situation where you should avoid having a window is over the bath, not simply because of the downdrop of cold air, but because it makes opening and closing something of a gymnastic feat. One interior designer, famous enough to have known better, performed the reverse feat and placed his clients' bath directly under an existing window, much to their subsequent chagrin.

If windows are not overlooked at all, what could be nicer than clear glass panes, so that the sybaritic wallower in hot water can enjoy a view of waving branches or scudding clouds to complete his pleasure. Unfortunately, most of us do not enjoy the neighbour-free conditions which make this possible, and the window must accordingly be screened during the daytime as well as at night. Frosted glass is ugly, but pale translucent blinds or curtains, venetian blinds or even something which partly obscures the view like hanging plants, or plants set on shelves built across the

window, all look attractive and do a reasonably efficient job of daytime screening. When the lights are on, you will want something with more weight and substance.

Internal bathrooms, with no external walls, are sometimes the only means of obtaining an extra bathroom in an area where space is tight, and indeed in new buildings this is a planning device quite often used now so that full advantage may be taken of peripheral walls for more important rooms. Naturally daylight has to be sacrificed here, unless the internal room is in a flat-roofed building (perhaps an extension) in which case a plastic, double-skinned dome can bring a beautifully pearly light flooding into the place below. A bathroom being built into an attic might be similarly equipped, but this time with an opening rooflight set into the slope of the ceiling.

Artificial light in a bathroom should perform two functions. There should be a main and central source which will flood the whole room with light and provide the bright ambience which I think is essential for dispelling early morning miseries. And there should be task lighting to serve the mirror where you make up, trim your moustache, shave and so on. For safety, both types must be switched with hanging cords or, less satis-factorily, worked by normal switches set outside the room.

A pendant light is not a good idea. You may bang against it with a wet arm or inadvertently splash it, so that the possibility of an accident, however remote, cannot be ruled out. Fixed ceiling lights with either glass or plastic diffusers are safer and will cast the requisite

all-over glow. If you are lowering a ceiling in a too-high room, plastic diffuser panels can be set into the new ceiling, or the ceiling itself can be made of some only partially obscuring material such as Formalux which is beloved of architects in commercial situations but ideal for domestic use too, with the light source concealed above. Or a normal-height ceiling can be fitted with recessed tungsten downlighters or recessed fluorescent tubes behind plastic diffusers.

When it comes to task lighting you may, if shaving is the only task likely to be performed in the bathroom, be content with a straightforward fluorescent tube, surface-mounted above the mirror. But more decorative effects are achieved by concealing the fluorescent tubes behind mirrors or baffle boards, and if intricate jobs with an artistic content (like applying make-up) are pro-posed, the light source is best mounted on either side of the mirror. Fluorescent tubes are perfectly suitable, and so are spotlights (though these might reveal more of your face than you wish to see), or wall lights of a pseudo-period design if it is an old-fashioned interior you are trying to create. Make-up mirrors in actors' dressing rooms are traditionally framed by bare light-bulbs, with the light shining directly on to the face and this gives an excellent light for applying accurate make-up. Now this form of lighting is being much copied in super-glamorous bathrooms. Glamorous it may be, but it is also extremely efficient.

1. These pretty windows are not overlooked to any extent, so a luxuriant fern hung in front of one and bottle-bedecked shelves built across the other do a perfectly adequate screening job.

2. Fluorescent strip lighting concealed behind a plastic diffuser strip in this bathroom designed by Jacek Basista for his own Victorian house. Note too the mirror tiles above the vanitory unit with its red laminate work surface and cork-faced sliding doors.

3. Peter King is another designer who has used a similar form of lighting in his own bathroom, but the surface of his vanitory unit, indeed the whole bathroom, is lined with pleasant, buff-coloured semi-glazed ceramic tiles.

4. Despite enjoying complete privacy from the outside world, this pretty bathroom is quite light enough to use during the daytime as the light filters through the pale scallop-edged blinds.

3

4

1

For a small bathroom where cost is of paramount importance, such niceties may sound frivolous. Look instead then at things like a diffuser-covered fluorescent tube with in-built shaver socket, or a medicine cabinet with integral mirror, shaver socket *and* fluorescent light. These are not particularly distinguished accessories, but they are functional, serve two or three or even four purposes without taking up too much room, and though not exceptionally cheap, they are excellent value for money.

Extraction

Internal bathrooms are required under building regulations to be fitted with an extractor fan, and normally this is operated automatically with the main light switch. There is a short time-lapse after the light has been switched off before the fan ceases to work.

Naturally this type of refinement is not obligatory in a normal bathroom with exterior windows, but it is a most desirable extra for two reasons:

It will help to dissipate smells, and all bathrooms where there is a lavatory will have them. A busy family bathroom which is used by a succession of people during the morning rush-hour will be a much sweeter place if a fan is fitted.

It will also help to make the bathroom less subject to condensation. Already, I hope, the room is well heated, which will do much to prevent this unwelcome and destructive phenomenon. It may also be fitted with enough warm, soft surfaces such as carpet, wood and curtaining to discourage condensation still further. Nevertheless, a brisk, hot shower is still likely to generate a considerable amount of steam which will moisturize on such cold hard surfaces as there are, and the one final deterrent will be an efficient extractor fan.

The fan may be fitted in either the window or an external wall, and there are several good-looking white plastic models available. In addition, where a window or wall fan is not practicable, it is possible to fit a ceiling version which extracts into a loft-space or void.

Noise

There are two sorts of noise generated in a bathroom. One is human in origin and can be a source of embarrassment and irritation both to those making it and those listening to it on the other side of the door. Even the sound of someone brushing their teeth, to mention a less embarrassing source of noise, troubles the delicate nervous systems of some amongst us. As to the other human noises, if the bathroom opens directly on to a hallway or corridor they can tax your gracious living aspirations to the utmost.

There are several remedies. One is to have a lobby between the bathroom and the public part of the house, such as is not uncommon in a lavatory. In a new bathroom, good planning may make this possible but it is not always so easy in a conversion or refurbishment. Built-in cupboards, lining the walls which adjoin either a bedroom or corridor will, as suggested on page 93, do a considerable muffling job. Even the fact that walls are lined with tiles or wood panelling will help and so will a quantity of sound-absorbing soft surfaces in the room, such as carpet, curtaining and acoustic ceiling tiles. At the very least, make sure you have a heavy, tight-fitting door through which the minumum of sound will penetrate.

The other sort of noise comes from the plumbing and the lavatory flush, which can be irritating if you are a light sleeper in the next room. The syphonic-flush lavatories mentioned on page 89 function much more quietly than the wash-down type, and are worth the extra cost if you seek peace. A talk with the plumber who is installing your pipes (or with the architect who is supervising his work) will help ensure that they are of the correct size and are securely fixed to the adjacent walls, for it is neglect of these details which could cause the night to be rent with banging and knocking noises.

1. **This small galley-shaped bathroom is shared by two bedrooms and has a door at each end. There is a sheet of mirror behind the wash bowl which is set into a laminated plastic surface, and lighting comes from silvered bulbs down each side of the mirror. The bathroom was designed by Pierre Botschi.**

2. **An extractor fan set into the window or an outside wall would be helpful if condensation is a problem.**

Materials

It will not have escaped your notice that many of the materials suggested as being suitable for use in kitchens have turned up again in this bathroom section. Not surprising, really. The same conditions prevail, to a large extent – wet, warmth and constant use. The difference is that the bathroom is a cleaner place, situated in the depths of the house and unlikely to be smeared with mud or splattered with grease. So whilst many materials will be mentioned in this section which have already appeared in 'Kitchens', there will be new ones too.

Floors

Bathroom users are often in their slippers, or barefooted, so the floor gets comparatively light use, apart from being splashed with water. Many people will find the hard, cold surfaces recommended for kitchens unfriendly here, and certainly their dirt-resisting pro- perties are superfluous, but for others their undoubted ease of maintenance and their convenience will be irresistible.

Boarded floor

This seems an unlikely choice for a bathroom, but there is at least one very successful example shown on this page, and in fact given the treatment recommended in the kitchens section – cleaned, sanded and treated with matt or glossy polyurethane – it does conform to all the bather's requirements. It is warm to the feet, will withstand some splashing and is not slippery. Used with large bathmats at salient spots, it would make a perfectly suitable and inexpensive if slightly unexpected bathroom floor.

Linoleum

Top-grade linoleum, as described in the kitchens section, is a possible material for laying in the bathroom,

1

1. This is far from being a run-of-the-mill bathroom in any way, and amongst other unexpected features is the boarded floor. Pleasantly honey-coloured after being cleaned and sanded, and then made water- and dirt-proof with several coats of polyurethane lacquer, it fits well with the austere and very sophisticated style of the room.

2. The production of cork tiles with a vinyl surface has made this material eminently suitable for bathroom use, and designer Jacek Basista has taken full advantage of the fact in his own bathroom, where they line the floor and the partition wall which conceals plumbing on the right. Note too that the screen which partially conceals the lavatory, and which holds books, plants and the lavatory-roll, also has a cork-tiled surface.

especially if the manufacturers come up with the good plain colours they have long been promising. But although its hard smoothness is fine for the kitchen, it has an intractable quality which some might find unattractive in the bathroom.

Vinyl

This, as described in the kitchens section, is an excellent material for bathroom use. The tiles would be particularly appropriate for laying in a small area since they would obviate the need to buy a great yardage of material, much of which would be cut away and wasted, and it would be a comparatively simple matter for even the most uncreative and cack-handed to work out a simple decorative pattern using tiles in two colours.

Synthetic rubber

As described in the kitchens section, this is a good material for bathroom floors. There is just one problem for those who suffer from tactile sensitivity. Most makes have a three-dimensional studded pattern which, whilst having excellent non-slip properties, could cause the odd shudder to those with squeamish soles. Otherwise it fulfils every requirement of the smart bathroom, including coming in a range of brilliant colours and being resistant to many chemicals.

Cork tiles

Cork tiles, both with a vinyl skin surface and without, have been described in the kitchens section, and the same advantages and deficiences (which are minimal) apply here. Natural cork tiles can be treated with varnish, but those manufactured with a vinyl skin, although they are more expensive, are perfectly splash-resistant without any further treatment. I think these tiles make a perfect covering for the average family bathroom.

Ceramic tiles

As already explained, there are difficulties – though not insuperable ones – involved in laying ceramic tiles on a suspended wooden floor. Bathrooms are often on an upper storey of the house, and so often have such a floor. In that case, due regard should be given to the extra work and consequent expense involved before using ceramics.

As I said before, there are two types, and whilst quarries might be suitable for the country-style bathroom, they have a homely, earthy quality that would make them inappropriate for a more sophisticated setting. *Glazed ceramics* on the other hand are slippery when wet, which in my opinion puts them right out of

1. Architect and designer Alan Tye has used brick-shaped buff quarry tiles to line both walls and floor of his very smart shower room. Note the cedarwood venetian blind, the dark-brown specially made radiator, and the bronze acrylic screen to the shower just visible on the right.

2. Carpet is a superbly warm and comforting floor covering for a bathroom, provided the room is not one which will be used by children or other notorious splashers. Here the very pretty blue carpet matches the blue-and-white tiles on the walls and bath panel.

3. This cloakroom was actually designed by architect Nicholas Grimshaw for use in a factory, but – always assuming you are up to the high tech ethos – would look dramatic and be very practical in the home. The walls are lined in stainless steel, the wash bowl and lavatory are made of stainless steel, the floor is covered in bright-green synthetic rubber and there are red door handles, lavatory-roll holder and ashtray. Stainless steel, used in this way, makes a splendidly reflective surface as well as being extremely hardwearing and never needing decorating.

court for a bathroom which is going to be used by children or elderly people, quite apart from any other merits or deficiencies.

Marble

Marble has been described in the kitchens section. It is best laid on a concrete sub-floor which makes it impractical for many upstairs bathrooms. Marble tiles only 3 mm thick, which are widely used on the continent and by knowledgeable designers here, are both cheaper and easier to lay than the heavy marble slabs which were traditionally employed for this sort of work.

Granite

This has properties very similar to those of marble, except that it mainly comes in solid, sombre colours.

Terrazzo

This is an expensive and luxurious material consisting of marble chippings set in cement and ground smooth. Purchased in small paper-backed sheets, it is laid directly on to screed or adhesive and when set the paper is washed off. It is available in a range of soft colours and can be laid in beautiful patterns, but this is not really a task for the DIY person. Any tendency to noisiness and hardness can, as with other hard materials, be overcome by using mats, and the only major disadvantage is its high cost. Like marble, it is at its very best when used in combination with under-floor central heating.

Carpet

Whilst quite out of keeping in the kitchen, this is perfectly suitable for the bathroom. It has every advantage. It is warm and quiet, soft and comfortable to walk on, non-

3

slip, comes in a splendid range of colours and designs and can be costly or relatively inexpensive according to the purchaser's requirements. It can even be cleaned so long as the soiling is not too heavy or greasy. For obvious reasons, carpets made of non-rot synthetic fibres are generally recommended for bathroom use, and in a room which is to be used by children or other uncaring bathers this is preferable. Nor need it inhibit the choice of design or colour since some of these fibres are made into rich and beautiful carpets. But I do not think careful owners of one- or two-person bathrooms need restrict themselves in any such way, particularly if they are aware of the limitations of a woollen carpet. Having used one for years in a family bathroom, complete with large bathmats but perfectly normal and unrepressed children, I can report no problems as yet.

The real problem area in a carpeted bathroom is around the lavatory and this is especially so when a low-level lavatory is used by men. Then, I do not think carpet should be fitted up close to this piece of sanitaryware at all. Instead, there should be an insert of some washable material such as vinyl tiling, cork, linoleum, etc. Specially shaped cotton or nylon mats are an unattractive expedient, but anything would be better than urine-soaked carpet.

Wall coverings

Practically any of the wall coverings that you are likely to put up in the main living area of the house can be used on the main wall surfaces in a bathroom, so long as the room is warm and well ventilated and there is no problem with condensation. Only vulnerable positions around the bath, shower and wash bowl need special care, and here a hard and impervious surface is best.

Paint

This must be applied to a good smooth plaster or plasterboard surface. It is at long last available in strong and dramatic colours – even in subtle ones too – and it may be used to great effect on bathroom walls. It is inexpensive and combines happily with other areas to which materials such as tiles and paper have been applied. Gloss paint has a rich, shiny quality which will emphasize strong shapes and make a foil for sculptural-looking sanitaryware, but it does have a tendency to run with water if there is condensation. Emulsion paint, which has absorbent qualities so that steam is soaked up, is not as easily washed as gloss and soap splashes or other minor stains cannot be wiped away without 'spotting'. An eggshell finish has a soft sheen, and combines the better properties of both.

Wallpaper

Wallpaper also needs to be put on a smooth surface, is another inexpensive covering and will absorb very small quantities of condensation without any problem, though will start peeling off if the room is really damp, and should certainly not be used in the areas vulnerable to splashing unless covered in a sheet of protective glass. Designs range from pretty to dramatic, small- to large-patterned, hideous to beautiful. There are colourways to suit any scheme and prices to suit every pocket. A completely reliable covering is *paper-backed vinyl* which will survive considerable doses of condensation if this is a problem which has not yet been overcome. Unfortunately neither patterns nor colour options are so extensive as with ordinary paper. But there *are* a few good designs to be found by discriminating shoppers, and these are generally more suitable for bathroom than kitchen use.

Tongued and grooved boarding

This was described in the kitchens section and its concealing properties have been mentioned several times in the book – it will cover walls which are *not*

2

3

smooth and ready for paint or paper. Well sealed with several coats of matt or gloss polyurethane varnish, or gloss painted, it is virtually impervious to damp.

Paper-backed fabric

Whilst not an obvious choice for bathroom walls because it will rot if persistently wetted, this should be satisfactory in a room where the condensation problem is utterly defeated, particularly in one which has the ultimate refinement of an extractor fan. Silk, felt and wool are all available on a paper backing and they do give a most sumptuous and luxurious feeling to a bathroom. Naturally, these fabrics should not be applied to areas vulnerable to heavy splashing.

Marble

Particularly in the easy-to-handle tile form mentioned on page 126, this makes a luxurious, if expensive, wall covering.

Laminated plastics

These were described in the kitchens section. The textured finishes which are not always appropriate for

1. Three different wall surfaces have been used in this very smart London bathroom belonging to James and Ann Pilditch. There is metallic wallpaper with a geometric pattern which is reflected in panels of glass that line the wall over the bath, and complementary tiles surround the shower and line the sunken area into which the bath is set. This use of several materials is perfectly satisfactory when, as here, each is carefully chosen for its relationship to the others.

2. and 3. A recently introduced range of laminated plastics offers interesting new design possibilities for the bathroom. It includes, left, Maxi-Graph, which has a gloss surface cut into by a matt grid (colours black, ruby, grey and sandstone), and right, Disc, which has raised glass discs on a matt background (in the same colours).

kitchen work surfaces could be used on bathroom walls, as well as the gloss or combined matt and gloss designs which are a fairly recent innovation. Colours range from pale to brilliant, and used imaginatively these plastics could help to make an unusual and easily maintained interior.

Cork tiles

These are as soft as plastics are hard. They come in several sizes, a variety of natural colours from pale gold to very dark brown, and may be applied all in one colour, or in a combination of two to make a simple design. They are warm to the touch, absorb condensation, would help with any acoustic problem and are reasonably priced. Plastic-coated versions should be used on heavy splash areas, but straightforward cork is perfectly adequate elsewhere. This is a material not commonly used in bathrooms – except by a few wily architects and designers – but it deserves to be more popular.

Glazed ceramic tiles

Perhaps the most practical covering of all. They can be used to tile the whole room, or in small quantities around splash areas, according to the style of bathroom which is required. Reasonably easy to put up by the DIY person, they do need careful alignment and grouting if they are to fulfil their waterproofing function and look their best. Coloured grouting – formed by adding a colourant such as Colourblend to ordinary grout – can be used with striking effect. It comes in black, red, blue, green, yellow and brown, which seems to cover every possible colour scheme.

Synthetic rubber

Synthetic rubber such as has been described in the kitchens section, and which is suitable for bathroom floors, is also being suggested by its manufacturers for wall application. It has several of the advantages enjoyed by cork, in that it has good acoustic properties, comes in a range of colours (bright ones rather than natural browns), and can also be purchased in tile form. However, its studded, three-dimensional surface would gather talcum powder and fluff, which though it could be vacuumed away might deter some very practical bathroom planners.

Mirror-glass tiles

These are available in several sizes and can be used as a practical, decorative surface for areas of the bathroom needing to be protected from splashing. Particularly attractive is mirror mosaic – tiny squares of mirror mounted on paper – which can be cut to any size

1. Modern tile designs are not generally very attractive (though there are exceptions), but it is possible to find pretty old tiles in junk shops. Usually only available in small numbers, they can be combined with plain modern tiles. 2. Brick-shaped ceramic tiles with a matt glaze cover every surface in this bathroom designed by Peter King, including the partition wall between lavatory and bath. There is a wall-mounted shower at this end of the bath and the partition wall also conceals its plumbing. 3. Barry Weaver chose dark-brown cork tiles for his tiny bathroom. And he made them darker with black woodstain, sealed them with lacquer and even wrapped them round the shelves to achieve this striking effect.

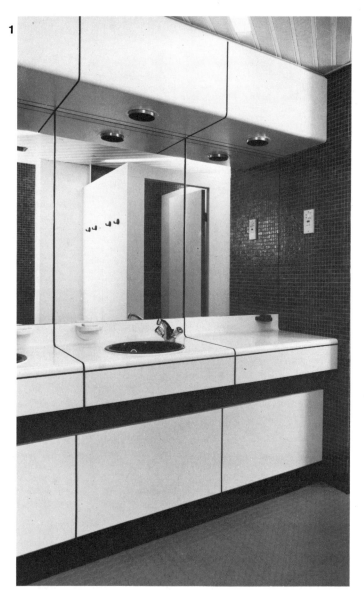

1

required and used in combination with ceramic tiles for decorative borders and inserts, as has been done most successfully in the bathroom shown on page 134.

Work surfaces

The 'work' done on bathroom surfaces is of a much less serious, taxing and dirty nature than the work done in kitchens. Nevertheless, the materials employed for these surfaces are likely to be similar, partly because both rooms have to contend with a considerable amount of splashing.

Laminated plastics

These are very often chosen, and with good reason, for their properties (as described elsewhere) are excellent for bathroom surfaces. Here, they should have post-formed edges whenever possible, both at the front of the

surface and at the back where it will curve up to meet the wall covering, thus forming an excellent waterproof joint.

The heavily textured designs are not really suitable for horizontal surfaces as they will cause bottles to wobble and maybe imprint their patterns on such delicate objects as make-up cartons or naked flesh.

Glazed ceramic tiles

These tiles form good bathroom surfaces, especially around a built-in bath or wash bowl, where soap and hard-water deposits are easily wiped away.

Marble

Marble is more suitable for the bathroom surface than the kitchen, where there is danger of it staining. The tiles mentioned earlier are particularly appropriate and more economical than slabs for relatively small areas such as a work surface.

Corian

A synthetic material available in opalescent white, or in several palely veined, marble-like designs. Its properties are unique and make it entirely appropriate for use as a bathroom work surface. It is immensely durable, stain resistant, non-porous and handsome. But, most interesting of all, though it is solid as marble, it can be worked exactly like wood, opening up possibilities for any manner of complicated and unique shapes.

It can be purchased as a ready-formed surface – with an integral wash bowl or bowls if required – or in thick sheet form for special working. Thin sheets, only 6 mm thick, are also available for wall cladding. Though it is expensive, the potential of Corian is immense, and has yet to be fully explored.

Hardwood

Hardwood can be used in the type of bathroom described on page 147, but it needs several coats of lacquer, such as is used on pub counters, to preserve it from the ravages of damp and soap splashes. Its installation would be work for a craftsman, rather than for somebody who likes a little weekend woodwork. Wash bowls are best set *below* this sort of work surface to avoid joints where dirt and damp could gather.

Granite

This is only likely to be used in a few rather masculine and expensive bathrooms. Its qualities are similar to those of marble, and it has an aura of massive permanence, so it is not the surface to be installed by those who like to change their decoration frequently.

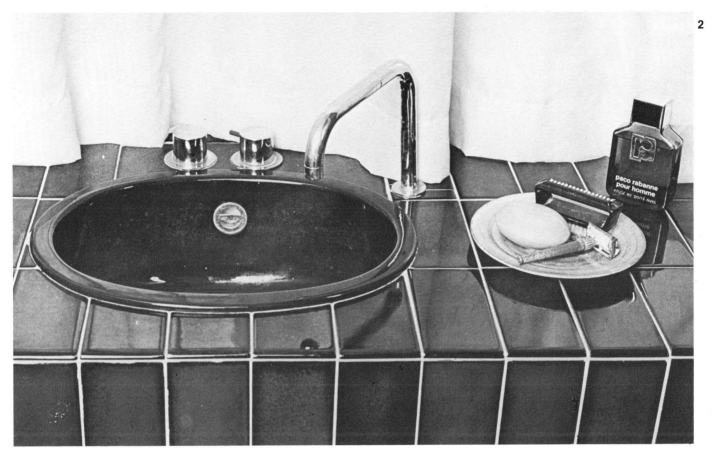

2

1. Laminated plastic, especially with a curved edge back and front, makes an excellent work surface for bathroom units and is available in a great range of colours, though patterned examples tend to be of poor design. The vanitory unit shown here was designed by Jeremy Rewse-Davies for the cloakroom of a suite of offices, but on a smaller scale would be equally suitable in a private house. Note the synthetic rubber floor covering.

2. Here the wash bowl is set into a shelf faced with brick-shaped, semi-glazed dark-brown tiles. Precisely laid and with white grouting, the tiles make a perfect foil for the dark-brown bowl.

3. Corian, a man-made material, with the appearance and toughness of marble coupled with an ability to be worked like hardwood, has been widely used in this sumptuous bathroom. It not only provides the work surface and upstand behind the wash bowl, but lines the raised platform into which the bath is set, and a large area of floor where splashing might occur. This bathroom illustrates well some of the potential of this new material in the home.

3

Decoration

1

There is a tendency amongst most home owners to treat the bathroom as poor relation to the kitchen when it comes to decoration. All enthusiasm and energetic shopping which goes into bedecking the kitchen fizzles out when it comes to the bathroom, and after an initial excited whirl into the world of coloured sanitaryware, the bathroom owner often leaves it at that, so that the result is a room which is relatively functional but lacks character or distinction.

The reasons for this difference are not difficult to spot. The kitchen is, emotionally and historically, the heart of the house, the woman's realm, the place where both family and friends often gather, so naturally it is the focus of much decorative effort and attention. The bathroom, on the other hand, is often used only briefly, not so often seen by friends, and certainly not the place where the matriarch holds court – not in most households, anyway. Similarly, with single people, social life generally stops short at the bathroom and it may even be regarded as a place where incipient loneliness or pernickety rituals become emphasized and depressing. So, if cash has to be cut and time, thought and careful shopping have to be curtailed anywhere, it is here.

What a pity, and what a mistake. The bathroom is, or can be, a place of refuge, relaxation and even inspiration. Plots can be hatched here, futures planned, dreams dreamed. It is the one place where most people enjoy utter privacy for a while – even if that privacy terminates with others banging on the door to get in – and it is the obvious and natural setting for a little fantasizing and self-indulgence. In the case of single people, any tendency to gloom or introspection will only be encouraged by a bleak and characterless bathroom, and the aim should be to defeat this at all costs.

Happily, the spaces involved are rarely so large as to make such decoration prohibitively expensive. Materials, however luxurious, will only be required in relatively small quantities, so that the odd sybaritic splurge on something as exotic as marble or thick-pile carpet will cause a quite minor financial lurch.

When you are planning the room, arranging the plumbing, buying the loo and making sure that condensation will never show its soggy face, keep in mind the fact that there is rather more to bathroom comfort than all that. Have a clear cameo picture in your mind of the style of room which will emerge at the end of your labours. What sort of setting is it going to be where you and others who use it will cosset yourselves away from the troubles and demands of the world outside?

Because bathrooms do not excite people's imagination and acquisitive senses in the way that kitchens do, the different types are not so pronounced, nor are they so many. Nevertheless, some people are instinctively creative in every detail and aspect of their lives, and as such they do not ignore the bathroom. If you have done so up until now, get set for a change. Here are some ideas which may help you to settle on a particular style of interior which will give you real satisfaction.

The country bathroom

This is likely to appeal to the people who have chosen a farmhouse-type kitchen, for it is the ablutive equivalent. As yet, though, its powerful charm has not been spoilt by over-popularization, and the examples one sees have a bucolic appeal and freshness which often belie the sophisticated plumbing and expert planning which have gone into their creation.

2

1. A very few simple finishes have been gathered together to produce a great sense of style in this small bathroom which was redecorated by designers Tony and Anne Barnes in their own home. White sanitaryware, white tiles, mirror mosaic and shaggy-pile white carpet have been assembled in such a way as to result in a lovely and tranquil room.

2. This country bathroom, belonging to James and Ann Pilditch, really is in the country, and it has all the fresh cleanliness of the genuine article. The sanitaryware is pale-blue and of large, old-fashioned dimensions, there is blue-and-white checked wallpaper and old wooden furniture picked up in local shops.

The country bathroom is nearly always a spacious one. If actual space is not available, means are found to create an illusion of it, for no element of tight-packed town living must interfere with the rural image. Despite that, the country bathroom is found just as often in the town as in the country, frequently having started life as a spare bedroom of some Edwardian or Victorian villa whose ample proportions lend themselves perfectly to this new use.

The country bathroom will look light and sunny, redolent of fresh air, and this will be intimated first of all by the colour-scheme. There will be none of those sludgy-coloured lavatories and wash bowls with which manufacturers have so enthusiastically crammed the showrooms in recent years. Sanitaryware here is likely to be white, with bright yellow accessories evocative of sunshine, or bright blue ones hinting at the colour of the sky over nearby meadows. Sometimes a country bathroom will have pale blue sanitaryware, chosen to suggest the requisite freshness and light. Unfortunately, this rarely works because the manufacturers' blues are not in the right shade range at all, and the faint grey tones which they manage to impart do nothing to evoke the country at all. No, white sanitaryware it has to be, but its shape and form and setting are as far as can be imagined from the clinical picture that it might summon up.

Sometimes the country wash bowl will be set into an old pine washstand which conceals its pipework and makes a pleasant and decorative substitute for that ubiquitous feature of the modern bathroom, the vanitory unit. The bath will be long, wide and deep, fit for a man off the moors or the farmland. If it is a modern bath, it will be boxed in with tongued and grooved pine boarding, though in the very best examples of the type it will be an old-fashioned shape, standing on its own legs (either a carefully restored original or one of the extremely expensive reproductions which are now available). Lavatory, bidet and shower will be equally lavishly proportioned. The lavatory seat will be pine rather than plastic, and although there will be plenty of storage in this room, it is not likely to be built-in. Instead it will take the shape of an old light wood armoire or chest. In the kind of household where there is no time or inclination for rummaging around second-hand shops in search of such treasures, it could well be a couple of free-standing pine chests or a cupboard bought from the local Habitat.

The floor will be covered in honey-coloured, plastic-coated cork tiles, and there will be big white cotton bathmats or, in less pecunious situations, rush mats, which thrive on a dose of water. There will not be many tiles, for these have incurably clinical associations, and such as there are will be prettily patterned (probably in blue or yellow according to the chosen scheme) and confined to a small splash-prone area immediately adjacent to the bath, shower, etc. The remaining wall surfaces will be treated with several coats of white gloss paint to reflect the sunshine or, if the wall surface is not good enough, panelled with tongued and grooved pine. The door too will be in pine, and all this unpainted wood will be treated with several coats of matt varnish to preserve it against the damp.

Full, filmy white or yellow curtains, preferably in fine cotton, will billow at the large window and for night-time there will be pine shutters or, a cheaper alternative, pinoleum blinds.

Taps will be Edwardian reproductions with a brass finish, but lighting will be quite simple and modern: a white glass diffuser to provide the main lighting, and something similar fixed to the wall on either side of the mirror. For simplicity is of the essence in this room. There will be few decorative accessories and no houseplants (an unnecessary intrusion in country rooms), just a simple wooden towel rack, lots of thick white towels and perhaps a bunch of fresh wild flowers in summer.

All the elements of this bathroom are perfectly easy to assemble. It requires none of the calculation, precision and rigid attention to detail which are essential for some other types. Even the plumbing pipes may, if well painted and not too dominating, show an occasional presence. Simplicity can though, paradoxically, be expensive to achieve and such is frequently the case with the country bathroom.

Bernard Hunt's bathroom is in London but it shows the way in which the country theme can be developed with pine storage cupboards, all woodwork stripped back to the natural pine and a blue-and-white window blind. White-painted walls and a white marble shelf containing two wash bowls, combined with a fortuitously bosky view from the window, make London grime seem worlds away, though it is in fact no further than the end of the road.

Architect's bathroom

This is a style which will be favoured by many of the best architects, both for their own homes and for clients who are sympathetic and enlightened enough to appreciate it. Not *all* architects will approve, however. A certain faction of the profession, debilitated and with enthusiasm undermined by public disapproval of its work in recent years, is suffering a crisis of confidence which has sent it bolting for the shelter of past idioms or, worse, some curious design fads which I do not propose to consider here. But the best architects have the courage of their convictions, warmed by their ability, and this is the style of room they will favour.

It will be a room of pristine tidiness, so naturally there will be built-in furniture, but not of the ready-made sort and scarcely apparent to the casual visitor. It will be concealed behind mirrored or panelled doors, hidden within the thickness of cavity walls, masquerading as a barrier between lavatory and main bath area. For this room, like the last, favours simplicity as one of its elements, but here the simplicity is of a most sophisticated and contrived variety. Smooth lines, unbroken runs of surface, a reliance on a great many precisely aligned tiles or immaculate panels of laminated plastics are a prominent feature.

The sanitaryware will be of as elegant and refined a line as it is possible to buy, plumbing might as well be non-existent for the amount that is on view. Nevertheless it is there, and functions perfectly. The sanitaryware will probably be white and if it is, this colour or non-colour will prevail throughout the room: tiles, floor, the lot. But the architect's bathroom may also be in a very strong colour-scheme, or in monochrome. For instance, there might be midnight-blue sanitaryware (made by one manufacturer only and not to be confused with a more glowing and vulgar blue), and matching tiles. With this there are likely to be bright red towels and red or navy blinds. Or the sanitaryware may be pale grey with a dark-grey-and-black supporting scheme, or shades of beige and coffee. But on balance, for practicality and aesthetic satisfaction, it will be white.

Every detail must be perfect in the architect's bathroom, and Alan Tye, architect and designer, who is the owner of the bathroom shown here, is a past-master in achieving such an effect. Not a pipe is to be seen, wash bowls (which he in fact designed) are set at different levels for children and adults, taps project from the walls and create no dirt-traps on the bowls, and the soft-brown tiles are beautifully set out and grouted. Note the easily-cleaned tiled bath panel.

All mirrors will be built in, frequently cladding the sliding doors which conceal cupboards, and whilst the bath will be in a boxed-out frame clad in tiles or laminated plastics, the wash bowls will be set under a beautifully smooth work surface clad in the same materials. The walls may be entirely covered in tiles of the predominant colour, and there could be a single horizontal band of contrasting colour around all four walls. The shower cabinet is likely to be specially made, entirely tile clad and of such depth and width that a shower curtain would be superfluous.

Some bathrooms of this type will have walls lined in panels of laminated plastics which will, need I add, be unpatterned, probably white and with no bad joints to spoil the streamlined effect. In the case of the navy-blue bathroom, the plastic may be in one of the new grid or graph patterns which is available in a similar colour.

Lighting will be concealed. Overall lighting will probably shine through a false ceiling specially constructed of light-diffusing plastic panels, or of white Formalux, and there will be fluorescent tubes built in and totally concealed behind cupboards adjacent to the main mirror. Taps will be of the Danish variety which are architect designed, with a white epoxy finish, and the floor will be covered in white vinyl tiles, except of course in the coloured bathroom where it will pick up the colour of the walls. An alternative floor covering is studded white rubber, which incidentally also makes a handsome textural wall covering and could be used there in place of tiles or plastic panels.

Towels may be on the thin and skimpy side, not because architects are too poor or mean to afford something better, but because bulky towels make untidy shapes which could spoil the pure lines of the room.

All accessories – lavatory-roll holder, toothbrush holder, towel rails, etc. – will follow this purist concept and be as smooth, well designed and unobtrusive as possible. There will, unexpectedly and dramatically, be one very large plant, lit to make a great shadow against the white walls.

This may be an internal bathroom. Architects are keen on maximizing the value of a small amount of house area by tucking bathrooms away in the centre of the plan. They are also addicted to plastic roof-domes, as

A silver-coloured venetian blind and chromed wire wall rack for storing bathroom belongings alleviate the starkness which a plethora of white tiles might have produced in Barry Weaver's small and precisely detailed bathroom.

described on page 120, when these are made possible by a flat roof above. But if there *is* a window it will be covered with either very narrow-slatted white blinds, or if it is a large one by slatted white vertical blinds. In any case these are likely to be kept partially closed during the day, throwing the interest back into the room.

Do not attempt this type of bathroom unless you are an architect or can afford to employ a good one, for its effect is entirely dependent on an exceptionally high and professional standard of design. Without this it will look commonplace and dull.

Filmstar bathroom

This, as its name implies, is an extraordinarily glamorous room, designed to succour the ego of its occupants, whether they be male or female. The decoration of this room will not be dramatic, for nothing must detract from the owner's image of his or her own charisma. Instead, it will be sumptuous, rich and flattering, a perfect foil, and a hedonistic setting for the ritual of body pampering and restoration which will take place there.

The filmstar bathroom may be large or small, but in either case there will be a wealth of mirror glass, partly to make the spaces appear even larger, but mainly because this material provides endless narcissistic reflections of the bather, as well as imparting marvellously dazzling and glamorous qualities at a relatively low cost. Much of it will conceal the floor-to-ceiling cupboards which are essential in a room where pots, jars, bottles, potions, medicaments, gowns and towels abound.

The colour scheme will be soft and flattering, in shades of peach and cream, soft greens, delicate pinks or light browns, because this is essentially a background room, and no element – certainly not bright colour – must detract from or compete with the personality of the owner.

The sanitaryware, to mention the most mundane component, will not be of simple classic design, but veer towards the lavishly shaped and voluptuous, with the bath often of double size, or an unusual shape and either sunken or set on a platform, both of which arrangements will contribute to the ritual of bathing. There is likely to be a jacuzzi or whirlpool installation to add to the hedonistic delights as well as help in combating cellulite. But though there will almost certainly be two wash bowls, a lavatory (probably in a separately partitioned area) and definitely a bidet, this bathroom is not likely to have a shower compartment. For this is not a family room, it will be used at most by two people and neither is likely to favour the brisk, brief and

stimulating properties of the shower-bath. As for hair-washing, well the owner of this type of bathroom will wash his or her own hair only when *in extremis*.

The floor will either be close-carpeted in a pale colour to complement the general scheme – cream, pale green or beige – with large fluffy bathmats, or it will be clad in pale, creamy travertine marble. If there are marble floors, the walls not covered by mirrors will be covered by marble too, and so will the vanitory shelf surfaces. If the floor has a simple carpet covering, walls are likely to be lined in paper-backed silk. This may be the ersatz variety made of plastic, but if money is no object, silk is perfectly feasible in what will of course be a heated and ventilated room. Work surfaces may be in polished travertine marble, though if an unusual and complicated shape is required – a probable eventuality in filmstar bathrooms – Corian will be much more amenable and look almost as rich and sumptuous.

Background lighting, contrary to the norm, will be soft and complimentary, probably from wall lights concealed behind peach-coloured glass diffusers, or from tungsten or fluorescent tubes totally concealed behind mirrors so that they merely cast a gentle glow on to the ceiling and walls. But when it comes to the make-up mirror, caution and self-delusion will be bravely cast aside. Here there will be the traditional filmstar lighting: a frame of bare bulbs around the mirror casting a frank and revealing glare over the viewer. And the owner of the bathroom will not hesitate to switch on these bulbs night or day in the quest for beauty. Daylight, though, will be treated in the same way as the artificial background lighting and gently filtered through ample folds of unlined white silk or Terylene. At night, silk ties will be released to let down lined silk curtains in a pastel colour or, alternatively, silk festoon blinds will drop down over the window.

This room is the very epitome of a filmstar bathroom. Pale-grey carpet is fitted throughout, pale-mauve silk lines the walls, and the wash bowls are set into gleaming white Corian surfaces. Mirrors line the walls and ample cupboards, and the bath is grandly raised on a Corian-faced platform. Soft overhead lighting is supplemented by the rows of very revealing bare bulbs which flank the make-up mirror. A bathroom such as this is not, of course, suitable for general family use, but certainly not as impractical as its appearance might initially suggest.

Taps, toothbrush holders and so on will be gold plated, towels will be large and thick and in a variety of pastel colours to suit the overall scheme, and accessories will be abundant. Lalique glass ornaments (or replicas looking uncommonly like them) will bask in the strong lighting of the vanitory shelf, along with expensive bottles of scent and the most glamorous of the lotion and powder containers. A large plant holder, built in below the window or at the end of the bath, will be overflowing with flowering plants whatever the time of year – pink African violets, white or pink poinsettias, creamy primulas, pale-blue streptocarpus, peachy hibiscus – and pure silk nightwear and robes will hang behind the door. A chaise-longue or elegant sofa, exquisitely upholstered in the same silk as lines the walls, will emphasize the inherent luxury of this room, though if space is on the tight side a low, curvaceously upholstered chair will make an adequate substitute, and there will be a rack or low table for glossy magazines.

There is likely to be a professional involved in the design of the filmstar bathroom. It is not easy to pack in all that glass and marble, raise or lower the bath, build the cupboards and conceal the lighting if you are an amateur. But when it comes to the choosing of colours, the actual positioning of the mirrors, and the general decorations, the owner will be much involved, for this is above all else a personal bathroom which no outsider can expect to complete to the last detail.

The basic bathroom

This is the most common bathroom of all, owned by huge numbers of people, and although it *can* be made gay and charming and comfortable, this is no easy task, for the existing components will often defeat even the most imaginative and ambitious of owners.

The basic bathroom is small, almost certainly in an estate house and it can be of any generation dating from the early thirties. If it is older than that, it is probably a small bedroom which has been converted into a bathroom at some time. The builder or converter, in an effort to beguile potential purchasers, has installed a suite of coloured sanitaryware with matching tiles halfway up the walls. Beyond that, it will be bleak, uninviting and without character.

This bathroom will never see a designer or architect, unless he or she happens to own it. It will be transformed with the aid of hard work, much thought, a touch of flair but comparatively little cash. Colour will be a major factor in this transformation, and expensive materials and components will hardly figure, though where they do they will be in such small quantities that, with minimal labour costs, the financial burden will be bearable.

An important feature will be the plumbing pipes. Some builders apparently like the look of them. In any case, they festoon them liberally around only too many rooms of this type, so a decision will need to be taken as to whether or not they should be concealed. In the very basic bathroom they will stay, for this is a room where there is no money and quite probably no space to build in cupboards, trunking or other concealing devices.

No. This is to be a paint job. Tiles, walls, ceiling, woodwork and pipes will all be painted, but there will be none of your prissy, pastel efforts. The paint used will be a good strong colour to give this bare little room the personality and presence it so desperately needs. Aubergine if the resident sanitaryware is that awful washy mauve colour; rich forest green if it is pale green; or black if it is white, are all possibilities. The pipework will be lost in the depths of these strong colours. The anaemically coloured, or worse still hideously patterned, tiles inherited with the room will take on new life under this drastic treatment, and the bath, lavatory and wash bowl will, instead of looking sickly, make a pale and pleasant contrast.

So will everything else in the room. If new light plastic taps can possibly replace the garish and cheap chrome horrors with which the room was undoubtedly endowed, so much the better. Likewise, that frosted glass windowpane must be whipped out instantly to be replaced by clear glass, covered in a plain white blind with a border linking it to the colour of the room, through which daylight can filter. Artificial light will come from a simple, plastic-covered ceiling light, with a fluorescent tube over the mirror.

The floor space in this room is likely to be minute, so the cost of introducing one luxurious element – fitted carpet, preferably white and long-haired – will not be high, and the benefits in terms of warmth, appearance and psychological boost on a cold Monday morning immeasurable. Taking the carpet up the side of the bath to cover the existing bath panel will give the room a further lift.

Those sets of matching accessories in either plastic or wood were just made for this bathroom, because there will be no room or money for expensive built-in storage or huge towel rails. But lavatory-roll holder, soap holder, towel rings, shelves, small wall cupboards, etc., can all be obtained in wood or in a splendidly designed coloured-plastic range according to your predilections. And these will contribute a coherent, 'got together' feeling to this small room. Towels will be in white for the aubergine room, pink or sharp yellow for the green room, and red for the black room.

Take one ordinary bathroom with fairly utilitarian white sanitaryware, cover the floor with fitted carpet, the walls and ceiling with a pretty yellow-patterned wallpaper, and install new light-fittings around the mirror over the wash bowl. This bathroom shows the attractive result.

Small though the place is, any horizontal surface – the window-sill, a wide bath ledge or shelves – will be crammed with small, healthy houseplants, and inexpensive prints and photographs in second-hand frames will decorate the walls. Starting life in the bleak, uncompromising fashion that it did, this room will have been coaxed into a striking, cheerful and welcoming place by its owners.

Period bathroom

It is not always exactly certain *which* period is being invoked in the design of this bathroom. Even the interior designer who is called in to do the job – for this is likely to be professional work – will probably not be absolutely clear, or if he is his clients will surely not let him cling to his purist principles. Let us just say it hovers comfortably between Victorian and Edwardian, with a bias towards

1. Despite its bold and handsome appearance, this basic bathroom was not expensive and depends for its effect on little more than the cost of a few pots of paint. Built in the 1930s when pale-green tiles were in vogue, it did not appeal to Dieter Klein, its new owner, so while retaining old sanitaryware, he painted ceiling and walls (including the tiles) black, added a tiny scrap of white fitted carpet to its small floor, red towels and blind and a black-and-white frieze. The result is dramatic, to say the least.

2. This period bathroom is quite different from the basic bathroom, relying on expensive mahogany panelling, antique brass taps and a charming blue-and-white patterned wash bowl for its tranquil charms. Here, too, there is fitted pale carpet, and a lacy white blind screens the window. This particular room was designed and made by Ron Cooper, and it certainly needs somebody with his skill to produce the desired effect.

2

the latter but picking out the most seductive features of each.

This bathroom, whilst not exclusively a male preserve, is far more likely to appeal to a man than to a woman, and is therefore most often seen in bachelor apartments. Here its proportions are small, but larger versions are popular in prosperous country houses.

Did period bathrooms have everything, including the walls, encased in mahogany the first time around? I am not sure that they did, but such is certainly the case in these latter-day incarnations.

Walls are heavily panelled, and incorporate a quantity of brass-handled cupboards as well as a huge, bevel-edged mirror. The bath is large and white and set into a mahogany-panelled frame, and the wash bowl, which may be a prettily floral-patterned reproduction of an antique bowl, is built into a mahogany surface. Some fiercely male characters may opt for the rugged magnificence of a polished granite surface, but mahogany is more usual.

The masculine influence will again be evident in the ample, strong lines of all the remaining sanitaryware, and in the colour scheme which will be limited to the rich brown and white predetermined by the wood and porcelain. Only the gleam of brass-finished Edwardian taps, brass handles, clothes hooks and other details will intrude upon the sombre richness of it all.

Curiously enough, there will be just one markedly feminine element in the room. This is at the windows. Two sets of blinds will hang there – daytime ones made of ecru-coloured cotton lace, and dark-brown Roman blinds (yet another period!) for night-time.

Artificial lighting will consist of Edwardian reproduction wall fittings with curly glass shades. These will be placed at strategic positions around the room, and two will flank the main mirror for close work. In addition to this main mirror there will probably be one of those charming pivot shaving mirrors on a brass or delicate mahogany stand.

Paintwork in this room will be pale cream gloss, setting off the brass accessories to perfection, and any wall surface not panelled in mahogany will be lined in felt in a different shade of brown. The floor will have close carpeting in a formal modern design in shades of brown and cream, because, unexpectedly, these geometric patterns look excellent against such a period background. Where the structure of the floor is suitable and there is a granite shelf surface, the floor may be laid to match.

Unfortunately, well-designed accessories like heated towel rails, lavatory-roll holders and soap dishes are not widely available in the requisite brass finish, so these will either be specially made or, more likely, towels will be hung on mahogany rails near the heating outlets, and everything else will be made of white ceramic and as discreetly situated as possible: recessed within the walls, or at a low level. Toothbrushes will repose in large white porcelain mugs.

There will be no tiling at all, but the mahogany will be treated with heavy lacquer, particular attention being given to vulnerable areas around wash bowl and bath to preserve them against warping and staining. And any area of felt-covered wall which might be in the danger zone will be covered in panels of clear glass, though this eventuality should not occur in a really well-planned room.

Towels will be huge, and in white or varying shades of brown, with the owner's initials embroidered on each one in black. There will probably be several beautifully shaped black glass bottles standing on the mahogany or granite shelf, containing the expensive pomades and shaving lotion favoured by this class of bathroom owner. Other accessories will be made of brass, lacquered to preserve their shine, and there will be one or two marine or hunting prints on the walls. Plants will not be much in evidence in this masculine room, save for the odd fern or aspidistra.

The period bathroom will be every bit as sumptuous as the filmstar type, but its glories will be partially obscured by a very deceptive, no-nonsense approach. Some women will enjoy such an ambience, but many will find it rather overpowering and leave it to the man of the house. For bachelors it will symbolize all the unencumbered and mildly self-indulgent elegance they hold so dear. This can never be anything but an expensive bathroom.

Once there were huge free-standing baths with claw feet. They took a considerable amount of hot water and, of course, they had to be cleaned – inside, outside and underneath. The time came when they were superseded by smaller baths, tidily boxed-in and with less area to clean. The wheel having turned full circle, one or two manufacturers are now making free-standing models again like the one in grp (glass-fibre-reinforced plastic) shown here. It makes a very handsome addition to a luxurious period bathroom and its elegant brass hand-shower fitting is a perfect complement.

The fitted bathroom

The fitted bathroom is more than likely to be owned by people who started out with aspirations towards an architect's bathroom, but who are held back by several considerations.

First, and most important, they haven't *quite* got the nerve to commit themselves to a room of such uncompromising and forbidding purity. They can imagine the look of supercilious surprise on the faces of their stodgier friends at first sight of this clinical masterpiece, and the way their local handyman will suggest ways of 'softening it up a bit, mate'.

In addition, they have not got an enormous amount of space, money is tight enough to be a powerful consideration, and you cannot leave *that* sort of room only partly finished, if you run out halfway. Anyway, they do not actually know a good architect, they are aware it takes time to search one out, that he will be expensive, the whole job will take months and that during this time the house will be in turmoil. No, all in all they are more sensible to settle for a fitted bathroom chosen from a proprietary range. They will then work out which of the modular units they want to complete the whole room, price them, and decide which they can afford to have straight away, postponing buying the rest until they have recovered their financial position.

The existing bathroom will be stripped out (or if the sanitaryware is good that will be retained but possibly repositioned) and, with the aid of that local handyman, who will be much more receptive to this style of interior since he is already familiar with its kitchen antecedent, everything will be fitted and installed within a gratifyingly short period of time.

The ready-made units chosen are likely to be in pale wood, for although the owners of this bathroom are keen on smooth, uncluttered lines, they like the warm look of wood (they are not *really* architect's bathroom people at all). If buying new sanitaryware they may select a light tan, which they feel will look smart against the pale colour of the wood. They will limit themselves at

Wood does not have to be kept to its natural colour, and this fitted bathroom has 'soft-limed' veneer of a most delicate and delightful blue. There is a white-tiled floor and wash bowl as contrast, lighting from inset ceiling spots, and a general feeling of well-controlled comfort. This is a large room, and it shows the optimum use of a top-quality fitted bathroom range in this sort of situation.

first to casing for the bath, lavatory and wash bowl and this will conceal most of the plumbing. The bowl will be set into a post-formed plastic shelf which is a part of the system, set over two units containing cupboards and drawers, and there will be no projecting handles because all doors and drawers open with recessed hand-grips. Later they plan to have floor-to-ceiling cupboards which will conceal the very last of their pipework, and a couple of wall units which they are going to need as the family grows. In the meantime, they will make do with the storage under the wash bowl and will be delighted that they managed to afford the large mirror with a built-in overhead light fitting which is all part of the system, and those flap-up compartments next to the lavatory for the lavatory-roll holder and cleaning brush. The main lighting in the room will be bright and warm, and will come from spots, semi-recessed into the white-painted ceiling.

There will be light-tan tiles around the bath and above the wash bowl, and the walls will be covered in paper-backed vinyl in a small, neat pattern which is a roughly similar shade. The owners of this room are basically extremely practical and cautious – as may be apparent from what has been said before – so there will be no extravagant floor covering, but good-quality vinyl tiles in beige, with a striking border in tan, and a wooden duck-board to stand on when they get out of the bath.

They like chrome fittings which look bright and modern, but since they care very much about the design of even such small accessories as taps, they will search out the very best looking ones they can find amongst the more conventional ranges; the handsome and less common designs which have been mentioned elsewhere are unfortunately too expensive. Towels will be in tan and beige stripes and hang on a large, heated chrome rail, there will be white blinds and tan cotton curtains at the windows, and the whole comfortable room with its gentle, mellow colour scheme will have any danger of blandness dispelled by a great basket of bright greenery hanging from the ceiling.

This bathroom will have been very cleverly and sensibly planned by its owners. It will not have been excessively expensive, or at least the expense will only have occurred in easy and carefully judged stages.

1

It is easy – well, comparatively – to sit down and write about how to make a successful bathroom and kitchen. It is sheer delight to go out and look at and photograph good examples; and those shown in this book are, I hope you will agree, both good and diverse. These were my tasks and I enjoyed them.

You, though, are now going to set about making such rooms for yourself (or at least I presume you are, for otherwise why should you have bought this book?). And that, frankly, is not nearly so easy. But everything written here is intended to smooth your path and make the whole project as enjoyable and snag-proof as possible oy telling you about the best products available, the most straightforward way to plan your layouts and choose your style.

One further point needs emphasizing. Don't rush. After many. years in the design business I have landed myself with the most unsuitable kitchen floor imaginable – the pale quarry tiles mentioned on page 59. Frantic to get the kitchen organized in our newly purchased house, I let myself be panicked into choosing them because they looked beautiful instead of taking time to carefully check over their properties. If I had I'd have discovered that because they are so absorbent it is virtually impossible to protect or seal them against oil and grease stains. I'm sure many people can recount similar disasters. So, however urgent your need to get the room into action, take each step carefully and without rush. Enjoy the process of planning and selection rather than being hassled by it. That way, you will avoid the pitfalls and have the best chance of ending up with a room that works well in every detail, as well as giving great visual delight.

1. This fitted bathroom has a pleasant beige-and-brown colour scheme which manages to detract from the fact that its curved, smooth-looking units are actually made of laminated plastic. All walls are concealed by the cupboard units, units which hold the lavatory, bidet, wash bowl and bath, and by banks of drawers. Note the recessed lavatory-roll holder, and the recessed shelves over bidet and bath. This sort of room does not have to be built all in one go – the various fittings can be acquired over a period of time according to the state of the owner's finances.

2. Details are as important in the bathroom as they are in any other room, and here is one in a delightful country bathroom belonging to James and Anne Pilditch. An old wooden towel rail, painted white, and hung with handmade white guest towels, is set against a white wall bordered with a blue-and-white frieze.

3. In complete contrast to the sophisticated fitted bathroom on pages 150–51, this one has been left in its natural state, with a pine bath panel and floor contrasting nicely with white sanitaryware and blue-and-white tiles.

Useful addresses

Manufacturers and suppliers

Bathroom accessories
Crayonne Ltd, Windmill Road, Sunbury-upon-Thames, Middlesex (Plastic)

Habitat, Hithercroft Road, Wallingford, Oxfordshire – and stores (Wood, wood and ceramic, plastic-covered wire)

H. & R. Johnson, Highgate Tile Works, Tunstall, Stoke-on-Trent (Ceramic)

Metlex Industries Ltd, Sumner Road, Croydon (Cabinets, linen-boxes and metal accessories)

Pilkington Tiles Ltd, Box 4, Clifton Junction, Manchester (Ceramic)

Bathroom and kitchen products for the disabled
Armitage Shanks Ltd, Armitage, Rugeley, Staffordshire (Sanitaryware)

Chiltern Medical Developments (Equipment) Ltd, 57 Southern Way, Thame, Oxfordshire

Clos-o-mat (Great Britain) Ltd, 2 Brooklands Road, Sale, Cheshire (Automatic lavatory)

Medic-Bath Ltd, Ashfield Works, Hulme Hall Lane, Manchester

Metlex Industries Ltd, Sumner Road, Croydon, Surrey (Bathroom products)

George A. Moore & Co. Ltd, Thorp Arch Trading Estate Wetherby, W. Yorkshire (Kitchen cupboards)

Parker Bath Developments Ltd, Queensway, Stem Lane Industrial Estate, New Milton, Hampshire (Baths)

Southern Sanitary Specialists Ltd, Unit K, East Portway Industrial Estate, Andover, Hampshire

Dishwashers
AEG (UK) Ltd, Bath Road, Slough

Beekay Bauknecht Ltd, 6 Priorswood Place, East Pimbo, Skelmersdale, Lancashire

Bendix, Thorn Domestic Appliances (Electrical) Ltd, New Lane, Havant, Hampshire

Robert Bosch Ltd, PO Box 166, Rhodes Way, Watford, Hertfordshire

Colston Domestic Appliances Ltd, Colston House, London Road, High Wycombe, Buckinghamshire

Creda Ltd, Blythe Bridge, Stoke-on-Trent

De Dietrich Ltd, Unit D, Houndmills Industrial Estate, Telford Road, Basingstoke, Hampshire

Electrolux Ltd, Oakley Road, Luton, Bedfordshire

Gaggenau Electric (UK) Ltd, Colville Road, London W3

Hotpoint Ltd, Celta Road, Peterborough

Indesit Ltd, 292 Streatham High Road, London SW16

Miele Company Ltd, Fairacres, Marcham Road, Abingdon, Oxfordshire

Philco GB Ltd, Heather Park Drive, Wembley, Middlesex

Philips Major Appliances, Lightcliffe Factory, Hipperholme, Halifax

Zanussi, IAZ International (UK) Ltd, Zanussi House, Reading

Extractor fans
Silavent Ltd, 32 Blyth Road, Hayes, Middlesex

Vent-Axia Ltd, Fleming Way, Crawley, W. Sussex

Vortice Ltd, Lyncroft House, Thames Street, Staines, Middlesex

Xpelair Ltd, PO Box 220, Deykin Avenue, Witton, Birmingham

Fitted bathroom units
Aqualon, J. T. Ellis & Co. Ltd, Crown Works, Wakefield Road, Huddersfield, W. Yorkshire

Kama, St George's Road, Weybridge, Surrey

Poggenpohl (UK) Ltd, 226 Tolworth Rise South, Surbiton, Surrey

F. Wrighton & Sons Ltd, 3 Portman Square, London W1

Flooring
Amtico, 17 George Street, London W1 (Vinyl)

Armstrong Cork Co. Ltd, Armstrong House, 3 Chequers Square, Uxbridge, Middlesex (Cork and vinyl)

Domus, 260–62 Brompton Road, London SW3 (Ceramic tiles)

Dunlop Semtex Ltd, Chester Road, Erdington, Birmingham (Vinyl and linoleum)

Fired Earth Ltd, Portland Road, London W11 (Ceramic tiles)

Hannibal Ceramics, Wardour Street, London W1

Lamacrest Ltd, Crown Works, Cold Bath Road, Harrogate, Yorkshire (Terrazo)

Langley (London) Ltd, 163 Borough High Street, London SE1 (Ceramic tiles)

Marley Floors Ltd, PO Box 499, Sevenoaks, Kent (Vinyl)

Nairn Floors Ltd, 50 Upper Brook Street, London W1 (Vinyl)

Vigers, Stevens and Adams Ltd, Leadale Works, Craven Walk, London N16 (Wood)

J. Whitehead & Sons Ltd, Imperial Works, Kennington Oval, London SW11 (Marble)

George Woolliscroft & Sons Ltd, Melville Street, Hanley, Stoke-on-Trent (Ceramic tiles)

Zanetti & Bailey Ltd, Ashley Down Road, Bristol (Terrazo)

Instant water heaters
Aquatron Showers Ltd, Radway Road, Shirley, Solihull, W. Midlands

Dimplex Heating Ltd, Millbrook, Southampton

Gainsborough Electrical Ltd, Shefford Road, Aston, Birmingham

Redring Electric Ltd, Redring Works, Peterborough

Sadia Water Heaters Ltd, Hurricane Way, Norwich Airport, Norwich

Triton Aquatherm Ltd, Triton House, Weddington Terrace, Nuneaton, Warwickshire

Kitchen units

Alno, 164 King Street, London W6

Arclinea UK Ltd, 12 Cheval Place, London SW7

Robert Bosch Ltd, PO Box 166, Watford, Hertfordshire

Bulthaup UK Ltd, 26–8 Church Road, Welwyn Garden City, Hertfordshire

Colston Domestic Appliances Ltd, Colston House, London Road, High Wycombe, Buckinghamshire

De Dietrich Ltd, Unit D, Houndmills Industrial Estate, Telford Road, Basingstoke, Hampshire

Eastham Burco, Thornton, Blackpool

Gower Furniture Ltd, Holmfield Industrial Estate, Halifax, W. Yorkshire

Greencraft, Ingatestone, Essex

Grovewood Products Ltd, Tipton, West Midlands

Hygena Ltd, PO Box 18, Liverpool

Ideal Timber Products Ltd, Broadmeadow Estate, Dumbarton

Leicht Furniture Ltd, Leicht House, Lagoon Road, Orpington, Kent

Miele Company Ltd, Fairacres, Marcham Road, Abingdon, Oxfordshire

George A. Moore & Co. Ltd, Thorp Arch Trading Estate, Wetherby, W. Yorkshire

Neff (UK) Ltd, The Quadrangle, Westmount Centre, Uxbridge Road, Hayes, Middlesex

Poggenpohl UK Ltd, 226 Tolworth Rise South, Surbiton, Surrey

Siematic UK Ltd, 11–17 Fowler Road, Hainault Industrial Estate, Ilford, Essex

Smallbone & Co. (Devizes) Ltd, Unit 3, Garden Trading Estate, London Road, Devizes, Wiltshire

Solarbo Fitments Ltd, Commerce Way, Lancing, Sussex

Stoneham & Son (Deptford) Ltd, Powerscroft Road, Sidcup, Kent

Whiteleaf, Goodearl-Risboro Ltd, PO Box 2, Princes Risborough, Buckinghamshire

Winchmore Furniture, Mildenhall, Suffolk

F. Wrighton & Sons Ltd, 3 Portman Square, London W1

Zanussi, IAZ International (UK) Ltd, Zanussi House, Reading

Miscellaneous

Cape Universal Cladding Ltd, Box 165, Tolpits, Watford, Hertfordshire (Rooflights)

Fordham Plastics Ltd, Fordham House, Dudley Road, Wolverhampton (Extra-slim cistern, slim cistern for duct installation, floor-control lever)

Nicholls & Clarke Ltd, 3–10 Shoreditch High Street, London E1 (Colourblend for coloured grouting)

Plastilux Ltd, Nelson Road, Nelson Industrial Estate, Cramlington, Northumberland (Rooflights)

Red House (Rooflights) Ltd, Houston Industrial Estate, Livingstone, W. Lothian (Rooflights)

Saniflo Transbyn Ltd, Benford House, Bury Street, Ruislip, Middlesex (Macerator attachments for lavatories)

Ovens and hobs

AEG (UK) Ltd, Bath Road, Slough

Agaheat Appliances, PO Box 30, Keatley, Telford, Shropshire

Beekay Bauknecht Ltd, 6 Priorswood Place, East Pimbo, Skelmersdale, Lancashire

Belling & Co. Ltd, Enfield, Middlesex

Burco Ltd, Rosegrove, Burnley, Lancashire

Cannon Industries Ltd, Gough Road, Bilston, W. Midlands

Carron Company, Domestic Appliances Division, Falkirk, Stirlingshire

Creda Ltd, Blythe Bridge, Stoke-on-Trent

De Dietrich Ltd, Unit D, Houndmills Industrial Estate, Telford Road, Basingstoke, Hampshire

Electrolux Ltd, Luton, Bedfordshire

Gaggenau Electric (UK) Ltd, Colville Road, London W3

Husqvarna Ltd, 10 Oakley Road, Luton, Bedfordshire

Merrychef Microwave, Merrychef Ltd, Cradock Road, Reading, Berkshire (Microwave)

Philips Major Appliances Division, Lightcliffe Factory, Hipperholme, Halifax, W. Yorkshire

Sanyo Marubeni (UK) Ltd, 8 Greycaine Road, Watford, Hertfordshire (Microwave)

Sharp Electronics (UK) Ltd, Sharp House, Thorp Road, Manchester (Microwave)

Thorn Domestic Appliances Ltd, New Lane, Havant, Hampshire (Moffat & Tricity)

TI New World Ltd, New World House, Thelwall Lane, Warrington, Lancashire

Toshiba (UK) Ltd, Toshiba House, Frimley Road, Frimley, Camberley, Surrey (Microwave)

Refrigerators and freezers

AEG (UK) Ltd, Bath Road, Slough

Beekay Bauknecht Ltd, 6 Priorswood Place, East Pimbo, Skelmersdale, Lancashire

Robert Bosch Ltd, PO Box 166, Rhodes Way, Watford, Hertfordshire

Burco Ltd, Rosegrove, Burnley, Lancashire

Caravell Freezers Ltd, 21–3 St Leonards Lane, Edinburgh

Colston Domestic Appliances Ltd, Colston House, London Road, High Wycombe, Buckinghamshire

Electrolux Ltd, Luton, Bedfordshire

Hotpoint Ltd, Peterborough

Indesit Ltd, 292 Streatham High Street, London SW16
Lec Refrigeration Ltd, Bognor Regis, W. Sussex
Miele Company Ltd, Fairacres, Marcham Road, Abingdon, Oxfordshire
Philco GB Ltd, Heather Park Drive, Wembley, Middlesex
Philips Major Appliances, Lightcliffe Factory, Hipperholme, Halifax
Thorn Domestic Appliances Ltd, New Lane, Havant, Hampshire (Tricity)
Zanussi, IAZ International (UK) Ltd, Zanussi House, Reading

Sanitaryware

Armitage Shanks Ltd, Armitage, Rugeley, Staffordshire
Balterley Bathrooms Ltd, Marlborough Works, Broom Street, Hanley, Stoke-on-Trent
Carron Co., Falkirk, Stirlingshire
Chloride Shires, Guiseley, Leeds
Fordham Plastics Ltd, Fordham House, Dudley Road, Wolverhampton
Forma, Victor R. Mann & Co. Ltd, Unit 3, Mitcham Industrial Estate, 85 Streatham Road, Mitcham, Surrey
Ideal Standard Ltd, PO Box 60, National Avenue, Hull
Leisure Bathroom & Kitchen Products Ltd, Meadow Lane, Long Eaton, Nottingham
Nordic Bathrooms, Nordic House, Lesbourne Road, Reigate, Surrey
Royal Doulton, Whieldon Road, Stoke-on-Trent
W. & G. Sissons Ltd, Calver Mill, Sheffield (Stainless steel)
Twyfords Ltd, PO Box 23, Stoke-on-Trent
Vogue Bathrooms, Bilston, Staffordshire

Shower units and enclosures

Chloride Shires Ltd, Guiseley, Leeds
Daryl Showerama, Daryl Industries Ltd, Alfred Road, Wallasey, Wirral
Dolphin Showers Ltd, Bromwich Road, Worcester
Fordham Plastics Ltd, Fordham House, Dudley Road, Wolverhampton
Forma, Victor R. Mann & Co. Ltd, Unit 3, Mitcham Industrial Estate, 85 Streatham Road, Mitcham, Surrey
Leisure Bathroom and Kitchen Products Ltd, Meadow Lane, Long Eaton, Nottingham
Nordic Bathrooms, Nordic House, Lesbourne Road, Reigate, Surrey
Showerlux UK Ltd, 52 Somers Road, Rugby, Warwickshire
Twyfords Ltd, PO Box 23, Stoke-on-Trent

Sinks

G. E. C. Anderson Ltd, 89 Henkomer Road, Bushey, Watford (Stainless steel)

Berglen Associates Ltd, 39 Claudius Road, Colchester, Essex (Stainless and enamelled steel)
Carron Co., Falkirk, Stirlingshire (Stainless steel)
De Dietrich Ltd, Unit D, Houndmills Industrial Estate, Telford Road, Basingstoke, Hampshire (Enamelled steel)
Franke A. G., UK Sales: 3–5 Swan Street, Wilmslow, Cheshire (Stainless steel)
Leisure, Bathroom and Kitchen Products Ltd, Meadow Lane, Long Eaton, Nottingham (Stainless and enamelled steel)
Prowoda, Headbrook, Kington, Herefordshire (Enamelled steel)
W. & G. Sissons Ltd, Calver Mill, Sheffield (Stainless steel)

Taps and shower fittings

Aqualisa Products Ltd, Morewood, London Road, Sevenoaks, Kent
Balocchi, at Spectrum, 53 Endell Street, London WC2
Barking-Grohe, 5-13 River Road, Barking, Essex
Czech & Speake, 6 Great James Street, London WC1
Danum, Peglers Ltd, Belmont Works, St Catherine's Avenue, Doncaster, South Yorkshire
C. P. Hart & Sons, Newnham Terrace, Hercules Road, London SE1
Holdmark Ltd, St Martin's House, St Martin's-le-Grand, London EC1
Ideal Standard Ltd, PO Box 60, Kingston-upon-Hull
IMI Opella Ltd, Rotherwas Industrial Estate, Hereford
Shavrin Levatap Co. Ltd, 25 Hatton Garden, London EC1
Vola, The Bath Studio, 332 Uxbridge Road, Hatch End, Pinner, Middlesex

Wall coverings and work surfaces

Sally Anderson (Ceramics) Ltd, Parndon Mill, Harlow, Essex (Ceramic tiles)
Arborite Ltd, Bilton House, 54–8 Uxbridge Road, Ealing, London W5 (Laminated plastics)
B. Brown (Holborn) Ltd, 32/33 Greville Street, London EC1 (Textured wall coverings including fabric)
Corian CD (UK) Ltd, Jaytee House, Enfield, Leeds (Man-made material with the appearance of marble)
Elon Tiles, 8 Clarendon Cross, London W11 (Ceramic tiles)
Formica Ltd, Coast Road, North Shields, Tyne and Wear (Laminated plastics)
Hannibal Ceramics, Wardour Street, London W1 (Ceramic tiles)
H. & R. Johnson Tiles Ltd, Highgate Tile Works, Tunstall, Stoke-on-Trent (Ceramic tiles)
Langley (London) Ltd, 163 Borough High Street, London SE1 (Ceramic tiles)

Perstorp Warerite Ltd, Aycliff Industrial Estate, Newton Aycliff, Co. Dunbar (Laminated plastics)

Pilkington's Tiles Ltd, Box 4, Clifton Junction, Manchester (Ceramic tiles)

Rye Tiles, 12 Connaught Street, London W2 (Ceramic tiles)

Sphinx Tiles, Bath Road, Thatcham, Newbury, Berkshire (Ceramic tiles)

Stoneham Masonry Co. Ltd, Millbrook, Southampton (Marble)

Textured Wall Coverings Ltd, 2/5 Benjamin Street, London EC1 (Textured wall coverings including fabric)

Vymura, ICI Paints Division, Wexham Road, Slough (Plastic and plastic-coated wallpaper)

J. Whitehead & Sons Ltd, Imperial Works, Kennington Oval, London SE11 (Marble)

George Woolliscroft & Son Ltd, Melville Street, Hanley, Stoke-on-Trent (Ceramic tiles)

Waste-disposal units

Kenwood Wastaway, Thorn Domestic Appliances (Electrical) Ltd, New Lane, Havant, Hampshire

Maxmatic, Bestobell Home Appliances Ltd, 240–42 Bath Road, Slough, Buckinghamshire

Tweeny, Haigh Engineering (Sales) Co. Ltd, Ross-on-Wye, Herefordshire

Waste King, Wynbourne Satoba Equipment Ltd, Wilec House, 82–100 City Road, London EC1

Wastrel, IMC Ltd, Harvey Road, Croxley Green, Hertfordshire

Waste compactors

Kitchen Aid Division, Hobart Manufacturing Co. Ltd, Travellers Lane, North Mymms, Hatfield, Hertfordshire

Thermador Compactor, R.E.A. Bott (Wigmore Street) Ltd, 72 Wigmore Street, London W1

Washing machines and driers

AEG (UK) Ltd, Bath Road, Slough

Beekay Bauknecht Ltd, 6 Priorswood Place, East Pimbo, Skelmersdale, Lancashire

Bendix, Thorn Domestic Appliances (Electrical) Ltd, New Lane, Havant, Hampshire

Robert Bosch Ltd, PO Box 166, Rhodes Way, Watford, Hertfordshire

Colston Domestic Appliances Ltd, Colston House, London Road, High Wycombe, Buckinghamshire

Creda Ltd, Blythe Bridge, Stoke-on-Trent

De Dietrich Ltd, Unit D, Houndmills Industrial Estate, Telford Road, Basingstoke, Hampshire

Electrolux Ltd, Oakley Road, Luton, Bedfordshire

Hoover Ltd, Perivale, Greenford, Middlesex

Hotpoint Ltd, Celta Road, Peterborough

Indesit Ltd, 292 Streatham High Street, London SW16

Miele Company Ltd, Fairacres, Marcham Road, Abingdon, Oxfordshire

Philco GB Ltd, Heather Park Drive, Wembley, Middlesex

Philips Major Appliances, Lightcliffe Factory, Hipperholme, Halifax

Other addresses

British Gas Corporation,
59 Bryanston Street, London W1

(Home service advisers can be contacted through local showrooms where the address of the regional branch of your Gas Consumer Council may also be found.)

Building Centre,
26 Store Street, London W1

and in the following cities:

Birmingham: Engineering and Building Centre, Broad Street, Birmingham

Bristol: Building Centre Bristol, Colston Avenue, The Centre, Bristol

Cambridge: Building Centre Cambridge, 15–16 Trumpington Street, Cambridge

Coventry: Coventry Building Information Centre, Department of Architecture and Planning, Tower Block, New Council Offices, Coventry

Durham: Northern Counties Building Information Centre, Green Lane, Durham City

Glasgow: Building Centre, 6 Newton Terrace, Glasgow G3

Liverpool: Liverpool Building and Design Centre, Hope Street, Liverpool L1

Manchester: Building Centre, 113/115 Portland Street, Manchester M1

Nottingham: Nottingham Building Centre Ltd, 17/19 Goosegate, Nottingham

Southampton: Building Centre Southampton, 18–20 Cumberland Place, Southampton

Stoke-on-Trent: Building Information Centre, College of Building and Commerce, Stoke Road, Shelton, Stoke-on-Trent

Consumers Association, 14 Buckingham Street, London WC2; **The Design Centre**, 28 Haymarket, London SW1; **The Scottish Design Centre**, 72 Vincent Street, Glasgow; **Disabled Living Foundation**, 346 Kensington High Street, London W14; **Electricity Council**, 30 Millbank, London SW1; **Royal Institute of British Architects**, 66 Portland Place, London W1; **Royal Institution of Chartered Surveyors**, 12 Great George Street, London W1; **Society of Industrial Artists and Designers**, 12 Carlton House Terrace, London SW1

Picture credits

Pages 6/7 **1** Design Council, **2** Cliff Jones; 8/9 Jessica Strang; 10/11 **1** Cliff Jones, **2** Electrolux Ltd; 12/13 **1** Czech and Speake Ltd, **2** Holdmark Ltd; 14/15 **1** Cliff Jones, **2** Cliff Jones, **3** Cliff Jones; 16/17 **1** F. Wrighton and Sons Ltd, **2** F. Wrighton and Sons Ltd, **3** Smallbone and Co. (Devizes) Ltd; 18/19 **1** Cliff Jones, **2** F. Wrighton and Sons Ltd, **3** Cliff Jones; 22/23 **1** Cliff Jones, **2** Cliff Jones, **3** Cliff Jones; 24/25 **1** Gaggenau, **2** Creda, **3** Neff, **4** Creda, **5** Electrolux, **6** New World; 26/27 **1** Sissons, **2** Prowoda, **3** Robin Crane, **4** Sissons, **5** Sissons; 28/29 **1** Electrolux, **2** Miele; 30/31 **1** Creda, **2** Miele, **3** Cliff Jones, **4** Electrolux, **5** Miele; 32/33 **1** Cliff Jones, **2** Shavrin Levatap Co. Ltd, **3** Holdmark Ltd; 34/35 **1** Vola Taps, **2** Cliff Jones, **3** Robin Crane; 36/37 **1** Robin Crane, **2** Robin Crane, **3** Robin Crane, **4** De Dietrich, **5** Robin Crane; 38/39 **1** John Thompson, **2** John Thompson, **3** Jessica Strang; 40/41 **1** Robin Crane, **2** Ken Kirkwood, **3** Jessica Strang, **4** Barry Weaver, **5** Robin Crane, **6** Robin Crane; 42/43 **1** Robin Crane, **2** Cliff Jones; 44/45 **1** Robin Crane, **2** Robin Crane, **3** Robin Crane, **4** Ken Kirkwood; 46/47 **1** Robin Crane, **2** Robin Crane, **3** Cliff Jones; 48/49 **1** Cliff Jones, **2** Robin Crane, **3** Cliff Jones, **4** Robin Crane, **5** Andrew Holmes, **6** Robin Crane, **7** Cliff Jones, **8** Cliff Jones; 50/51 **1** Ken Kirkwood, **2** Cliff Jones, **3** Cliff Jones; 52/53 **1** Robin Crane, **2** Robin Crane, **3** Robin Crane; 54/55 **1** Cliff Jones, **2** Cliff Jones; 56/57 **1** IPC, **2** Cliff Jones; 58/59 **1** Cliff Jones, **2** Carl Freudenberg and Co. (UK) Ltd, **3** Jessica Strang; 60/61 **1** Jessica Strang, **2** Cliff Jones, **3** Peter Bell, **4** Cliff Jones; 62/63 **1** Susan Griggs Agency, **2** Author's collection, **3** Schiffini; 64/65 **1** Cliff Jones, **2** Cliff Jones, **3** Cliff Jones; 66/67 **1** Richard Einzig, **2** Cliff Jones; 68/69 **1** Cliff Jones, **2** Smallbone and Co. (Devizes) Ltd; 70/71 **1** Susan Griggs Agency, **2** Cliff Jones; 72/73 **1** Cliff Jones, **2** Richard Einzig; 74/75 **1** Cliff Jones; 76/77 **1** Cliff Jones, **2** Barry Weaver; 78/79 Jessica Strang; 80/81 **1** John Brookes, **2** Cliff Jones, **3** Cliff Jones; 82/83 **1** Cliff Jones, **2** Cliff Jones, **3** Cliff Jones; 84/85 **1** Vogue Bathrooms, **2** Twyfords; 86/87 **1** Cliff Jones, **2, 3, 4, 5** Ideal Standard; 88/89 **1** Robin Crane, **2** Vogue Bathrooms, **3** Czech and Speake Ltd, **4** Royal Doulton; 90/91 **1** C. P. Hart and Sons, **2** Cliff Jones, **3** Robin Crane, **4** Ideal Standard, **5** Ideal Standard, **6** Sissons, **7** Transbyn Ltd; 92/93 **1, 2, 3** Royal Doulton, **4** Poggenpohl UK Ltd; 94/95 **1** Royal Doulton, **2** Cliff Jones; 96/97 **1** Habitat, **2** Habitat, **3** Crayonne, **4** Robin Crane; 98/99 Cliff Jones; 100/101 **1, 2, 3, 4** Ken Smith, **5** Robin Crane; 102/103 **1** Robin Crane, **2** Robin Crane, **3** Cliff Jones; 104/105 **1** Twyfords, **2** Royal Doulton, **3** Armitage Shanks, **4** Cliff Jones, **5** Robin Crane; 106/107 **1** Robin Crane, **2** Cliff Jones; 108/109 **1** Redring Electric Ltd, **2** Walker Crosweller and Co. Ltd, Cliff Jones; 110/111 Cliff Jones; 112/113 **1** Forma, **2** Forma, **3** Cliff Jones; 114/115 **1** Cliff Jones, **2** Walker Crosweller, **3** Walker Crosweller, **4** Forma; 116/117 **1** Robin Crane, **2** Given by owner; 118/119 **1** Cliff Jones, **2** Cliff Jones; 120/121 **1** Robin Crane, **2** IPC, **3** Cliff Jones, **4** C. P. Hart; 122/123 **1** Ken Kirkwood, **2** Xpelair; 124/125 **1** Cliff Jones, **2** IPC; 126 **1** Ken Kirkwood, **2** Designer's Guild, **3** Nicholas Grimshaw; 128/129 **1** James and Ann Pilditch, **2** Formica Ltd, **3** Formica Ltd; 130/131 **1** Philippa Lewis, **2** Cliff Jones, **3** Barry Weaver; 132/133 **1** Jeremy Rewse-Davies, **2** Jessica Strang, **3** Cliff Jones; 134/135 **1** Ken Kirkwood, **2** Monica Amstad; 136/137 Cliff Jones; 138/139 Ken Kirkwood; 140/141 Angelo Hornak; 142/143 Cliff Jones; 144/145 Monica Amstad; 146/147 **1** Cliff Jones, **2** Susan Griggs Agency; 148/149 Cliff Jones; 150/151 Poggenpohl UK Ltd; 152/153 **1** Aqualon fittings by J. T. Ellis and Co. Ltd, **2** Monica Amstad, **3** Hunt Thompson Associates.

The two cover photographs are by Peter Williams. The front shows taps designed by Arne Jacobsen, manufactured by Vola and available from Heals, Tottenham Court Road, London WC1. The back shows shower taps and mixer in brass, available from Classy Brass, 65A New King's Road, London SW10. The blue Delft tiles are available from World's End Tiles and Flooring Ltd, 9 Langton Street, London SW10.

Index